Pick Up Stuff

Family Farm Life

by

Ernie Ranly

PublishAmerica
Baltimore

First printing

PublishAmerica has allowed this work to remain exactly as the author intended, verbatim, without editorial input.

Chapter 33, "Magdalen" appeared in a modified form in Commonweal. (Commonweal Foundation. 475 Riverside Drive. Room 405, New York, NY)

Looking for God's Country. Poems by Norbert Kraft. (Time Being Books: St. Louis Missouri, 2005).

ISBN: 978-1-4489-5307-3
PUBLISHED BY PUBLISHAMERICA, LLLP
www.publishamerica.com
Baltimore

Printed in the United States of America

How can one not dedicate this account of family life to Mom and Dad, to Brothers and Sisters.

And then to one Sister more, Ethel Gintoft, who in editing and re-editing the text has deeply shared these experiences and many more.

- A re-editing and collaboration by Genevieve Ritzel.
- We acknowledge two printings of this book by Messenger Press, Carthagena, Oh.

…You will never feel lost no matter how far you stray. As long as you remember, where you came from, and never forget that those who came before you where your family lives will always remain God's Country.

"God's Country"
Norbert Kraft

CONTENTS

Introduction

Before one could sweep in the Ranly house, someone had to pick up stuff.

The sitting room would be cluttered with unmatched shoes, children's toys, zipple caps (now we call them stocking caps), dominos and the like. Usually a little kid was assigned the task to pick up stuff, because she could crawl under the table, recover a shoe from Grandma Lamm's rocking chair and, lying flat on her stomach, could reach that last red poker chip under the sideboard.

This series of accounts is about my stuff.

I was fourteen years old when I left home in August, 1944. So my experiences and memories are quite specifically focused on a ten-year time frame, from about 1935 until 1944. The fact that I write about my stuff after some sixty years and from Lima, Peru, means that what I have to say is perfectly, authentically mine, but in many places I may be technically wrong. I am sorry about that.

By no stretch of the imagination am I a farmer or am I the one to explain how things work. What I am trying to do is to put into my words the way it was, the way we did it, the way the Ranly family did it, the way the Ranly family talked about it.

Nor is this a generalization about rural life in the late '30's. Other families may not recognize their own experiences here. Our family was something else. At times visitors—we called visitors "company"—told us: "You talk funny." Our "funny talk" was not only the many Germanisms from our immediate linguistic heritage (such as "zipple" cap), but we used some common words in uncommon ways. For example, we cooked and ate in the kitchen, lived and played in the sitting room and reserved the front room for company. There was no dining room, no living room, no patio, no breezeway. Mostly, everything took place in the sitting room. I guess maybe you could call it the family room.

That is why to sweep the sitting room, first someone had to pick up stuff. So here you have some of the stuff I've picked up along the way.

We start with Mom's birthday because, well, that's a good place to start. In the calendar year there is Mother's Day, and we did sing about "that little old red shawl my Mother wore." But for us kids, Mother was Mom with all the respect, love, tenderness, fun, and gratitude that our German Catholic heritage would allow us to express. So it was after Mom's birthday that we invite you to follow the seasons with us.

Ernie Ranly

1.
Mom's Birthday

May 11 was Mom's birthday. The cyclical return of the seasons centered around this date like a May pole.

May 11 was New Year's Day, Christmas, Easter and a common birthday for all of us. Because on Mom's birthday we were allowed to go barefoot!

The date was permanently marked on our calendars, seemingly since time immemorial. "Mom's birthday, first day to go barefoot." I have no idea when it began.

Late spring weather in western Ohio was not exactly programmed. Some years it was quite hot by the middle of April. Crocuses and daffodils were long out of bloom. The winter wheat was a dark green, like the color of the carpet undertakers throw over the bare ground of a recently dug grave. The oats were already sowed and much of the corn ground was already worked for planting. But could we go barefoot? Not before May 11! "I'll tell Mom!" Furtively, we'd sneak off our shoes in the soft grass by the chicken coop near the horseshoe pits. Until some one caught us.

Or the next year, spring would come late. I remember when Hilda married Florus Obringer on May 1, 1942. (This was also our parents' wedding anniversary.) The day was clear with a golden bright sun, but so cold there was frost on the ground, and particles of thin blue ice clung to the creek banks.

But whatever the temperature on May 11, off came the shoes for at least a fast run across the front lawn. Yet we ran carefully, gingerly, that first day. How tender the feet became, wrapped in socks and tied up in shoes since Labor Day (the start of school) until May 11, Mom's birthday.

By September we could race barefoot over gravel without wincing, the bottoms of our feet as tough as shoe leather.

Shoes may be convenient, even necessary, but shoes are artificial and restrictive. As the poet, Father Gerald Manley Hopkins put it: "nor do feet feel being shod."

Several of my sisters share with me a distaste for shoes. Indoors, all year round, we can very well go unshod, except for social pressures. As the song goes: "Put your shoes on Baby, don't you know you're in the city?"

Mom always complained that since Mother's Day was so close to her birthday and within a fortnight of our parents' wedding anniversary she was cheated out of several parties in her honor. She was right, of course, because we always conspired to have only one family party.

I see now that in those days, with our German heritage, we were not so very expressive of our emotions. But we were deeply sincere and honest, and I think it was in the clean hard fun we had that we loved Mom most. Today when I see my grand nephews and nieces show their open, warm love to their parents and grandparents I am so happy that some things DO change.

Life is a juncture of many things. Over the years, as a priest at the altar, I pray for Mom on her birthday. I am flooded with memories of tender feet caressing soft green grass. In a faith world where the Word of God is born of a village maid, I guess the memories of bare feet are not so outrageous during the Eucharist.

How else can I remember Mom's birthday?

2.
Wash Days

Monday was not necessarily wash day. In fact, it was usually Tuesday or Wednesday. Wash day began the night before as we gathered our dirty clothes. When we left for school on the morning of wash day, piles of clothes were lying all around, separated into whites, towels, bedding, colored clothes and really dirty clothes, like overalls.

Mom demanded that there be two big tubs of rain water standing by the washing machine by early morning on wash day. Earlier, washing was done in the smoke house with a gasoline motor on the Maytag washing machine. I remember best when the washing was done in the closed front porch with an electric motor on the Maytag.

We had several large tin tubs and one large wooden tub used for rinse water, which was always set aside of the washing machine. This same wooden tub was also used on butchering days for mixing the ground meat for sausage. We hauled the rain water from the cistern behind the house by the smoke house or from the well south of the house. The cistern had a tin pump we worked by pulling the center handle up and down like a butter churn. The well south of the house had a rusty heavy pump. Its wooden handle had always been broken. I see that same broken handle on that same old pump every time I am home.

Drinking water came from the drilled well under the wind pump. It was hard water, filled with chemicals and at times quite rusty. So, of course, it could not serve for washing water. During very dry summers the cistern would go dry. Then we had to buy truck-tanks of soft water. The trucks backed up past the back porch and poured the soft water into the cistern.

So after supper on the day before wash day an extra chore was carrying the rain water to the washing machine. We needed to set the wooden tub on top of a small wooden bench, next to the wringer of the washing machine.

The job took two people. It may seem simple enough. First, we pumped and pumped to fill the tubs from one of the two wells, using one of those distinctive hand pumps. Then two people, working as a team, lifted the tub by its two handles on the opposite sides of the tub so that they could walk off with the tub of water.

But pay a little attention here. If you lift your side a little higher than your partner's side, "accidentally" some water will splash over his/her feet. If the other person lifts his/her side higher than yours, you have to defend yourself, lifting your side even higher. How often did we come running alongside the house, carrying a full tub of water at the level of our heads! Mom would watch us and heave a big sigh.

As I have noted, Maytag was the trademark of our washing machine to the extent that we talked only about the Maytag. In the smoke house it worked with a puffing, chugging, smoking gasoline motor. After we got electricity in 1936 the Maytag had its own motor with a cord that we plugged into a socket on the wall.

The hum of the motor, with the peculiar rhythm of the washer, created a background music which set a sort of mood, an environment, a special sense of a special day. It was wash day.

The wringer was the focus of our unending curiosity. We watched the process with a sense of awe. Mom would slip the tip of a blue shirt in the rollers and the whole shirt would be sucked up into its jaws, the hot steamy soapy water falling back into the washer. Sometimes when Mom wasn't looking, we dared to stick a finger between those white heavy rollers. But we pulled it out immediately. We heard stories about children having their whole hand and arm being pulled into a wringer. We kept our distance.

The clotheslines were two heavy wires stretched out over steel posts permanently embedded in cement along the full length of the lawn by the hog lane. Our wash baskets were those light woven matted baskets that we brought home in late August full of Georgia peaches for canning. The wire handles cut into our hands when carrying a heavy load of wet wash. Before hanging the clean wash (we seldom called it laundry) we had to run a damp cloth up and down the wire lines to remove dust and bird droppings. The wooden clothespins were kept in a cloth bag with an open hole on one side, attached to a wire clothes hanger that slid up and down the clothes lines.

White sheets and pillow slips were always hung up first at the north end of the lines, nearest the house. Then dress shirts, dresses, underwear, stockings and finally the colored clothes. This, of course, was the order of washing. Extra steel posts had to be set up to help support the weight of our family wash. The two lines would be full all the way up to the hog stable.

Our lane is almost a fifth of a mile long. But cars passing by on the gravel road could see very well when the Ranlys had wash day. Walking home from school we saw the sheets flapping in the wind like white sails. The girls knew they had lots of ironing to do.

On bitter cold days, the wet wash would freeze stiff before it dried. But it was always hung outside for the fresh air. We had great fun when the frozen wash was brought into the house. A frozen suit of longjohns looked like a walking ghost.

Rain on wash day created chaos. We came home from school to find the sitting room covered with drying laundry. The collapsible wooden dryer, set up in full height next to the heating stove could take on only a small part of the wash. The rest was stretched out over the backs of chairs and on Grandma Lamm's rocker in the sitting room. The stove would be well stoked and blazing away. The air was hot but damp. Yet there was a pleasant smell of soap and cleanliness in the air.

Mom supervised the making of our own homemade soap. We saved all frying and grease droppings. I do not understand the chemistry of how a few cans of lye transformed all this mess into a light brown soap which was then cut up into manageable hand bars. I remember cardboard boxes of Oxydol. I think Mom used homemade soap for the heavy wash and store-bought soap for the finer articles. She probably made her own mix of the two kinds of soap.

The tradition of homemade soap gave my brother Art one of his famous lines in German: "Wir müssen heimgehen um Seife kuchen." "We have to go home to make soap." More literally, "to cook soap." This was the pretext visitors used to take early leave while visiting relatives or friends. "We have work to do, so, excuse us please, we must go home." Art always enjoyed the line.

Before electricity and electric irons, we had little iron plates which were put over the gas burners of the kitchen range. Then the flame was set very low and the clothes iron was placed upon the plate to heat. I watched Mom and my sisters lift up an iron, wet their fingers on their lips and test carefully the temperature of the iron before setting it down upon a white shirt. Yet we boys complained bitterly when we found a brown spot burned into our clothes with the exact outline of that clothes iron. Little did we pity the poor people who had to iron clothes with that type of iron.

I want to borrow an image I read in a book by Kathleen Norris. The angel of death comes into the house and taps the housekeeper on the shoulder, with the gesture that it's her time to go. And the housekeeper says—like, I am sure, Mom would have said—"You will just have to wait. First I must finish the ironing, fold the clothes and put away the wash."

3.
The Creek

In the dictionary it is spelled CREEK and the diacritical marks dictate that it is to be pronounced like the CREAK of a rocking chair. But in the local patois it is pronounced as if it were spelled CRICK, like the sound of tick-tock-tick. For us this little stream of water coming in from the southwest, then running from south to north, under the bridge in the lane and then on below Lookout Mountain was the CRICK. No self-respectable citizen would pronounce it publicly in the way it is spelled.

A watershed is a technical geological term and can have rather dramatic connotations. As a geographical fact, the state of Ohio makes an interesting study of watersheds. Rivers in the north (such as the Maumee) flow north into Lake Erie (and eventually into the Saint Lawrence and out to the North Atlantic). Waterways in the center and south of the state find their way into bigger streams, like the Miami or the Wabash Rivers, join up with the Ohio River, which, of course, is part of the Mississippi water system, and all the waters flow on to New Orleans and the Gulf of Mexico. The little geographical area that made up the parish and the school district of Cassella, Ohio, falls within the vagaries of such watersheds.

European settlers found the land below the dark forests to be wet, swampy, infested with mosquitoes and flies and very unhealthy. Many died young. After clearing the trees they found ways of draining the swampy areas by laying lines of red clay tiles, some two feet below the surface.

The tiles differed in circumference, from small ones of three/four inches, to large tiles, as big as ten/twelve inches across. Every tile was some fifteen inches long. They were laid end to end, with a small crack between two tiles. The tiling ditch had a slight fall so that as the water seeped through the cracks and entered into the causeway inside the tiles it flowed either into a bigger tile line or it led directly to an open canal or to a natural water way, such as our creek.

In early spring the farmers watched how the water gathered in low spots after heavy rains. Then they calculated where to lay new tile lines. The tiles were deep enough below the surface so that normal ploughing, disking, harrowing, planting would pass over the top of the tiles. (It was not unusual that a deep plough furrow might break open a tile line. This needed immediate repair.) Good drainage meant that the low ground could be worked three to four days earlier in the spring when time was of the essence to plant oats, corn and soy beans as soon as possible. And after planting it was crucial that the water from recent rains would not stand too long and drown out new seedlings.

I understand that now they use long plastic tubes with small holes for the water to seep through in place of the individual tiles. But the logic of the system is the same. It is highly functional.

I can remember on our own land at least six open tiles which fed into our creek. An open tile often received a steel trap during trapping season. We might catch anything at the mouth of a tile, from rabbit, muskrat, opossum to skunk. One time, we think we snagged a fox that got away.

As an open waterway, our creek began less than a mile from our land, originating from several neighbors' tile lines. So in itself, the creek was a very small body of water. Through the long hot summers it practically dried up.

But after days of steady rains or after a particularly heavy cloud burst, brown run-off waters would come rushing from several different directions. From the east and south, it ran off Strukamp's place along the highway, passed by the cane press, turned at the big poplar cottonwood tree on our land, and ran down into the creek. The water from the west was run off from the Kramer farm and came crashing through the catalpa grove and the lower orchard. The water from the east and the north came from the Ashman farm and Kempers' place.

The lane bridge was a hundred percent secure with its two high cement walls and its rusty iron beams. But when the water began lapping at the iron supports, Dad and the older brothers took out the wooden planks so that the force of the water would not take them downstream.

High water was very exceptional. Normally, our creek was a tame, domesticated thing, like another household pet. It was ours to wade in, to build small dams and spillways, to watch muskrats swim and dive into their underground burrows. The creek's banks were covered with poplar and willow trees where red-winged blackbirds frisked about, shouting out their sharp clear cries. We knew the places where we found wild strawberries in spring and blackberries in the dead of summer.

Along the creek in the field behind the orchard there was a mulberry tree. Its fruit became ripe around the middle of August. We carried an old but clean bed sheet to the bottom of the mulberry tree. An older boy climbed the tree and indicated to us where to spread the sheet. We stood there holding the sheet by its four corners. Then the kid in the tree began to shake just those few branches directly over the bed sheet. The ripe mulberries fell in a shower of blue-red-purple hail stones. Carefully we gathered together the four corners of the sheet, shook the berries into a pile and poured them into a steel galvanized milk bucket.

Of course, we ate the ripest, the juiciest of the mulberries. Our hands turned blue, our lips looked like clowns' mouths with dark purple stains. A second branch of the tree was selected. We repeated the process until we had a full bucket of lusciously soft blueberries.

Mom would bake them into pies for supper. We poured fresh cow's milk over the piece of pie and savored it as pure heaven on earth.

The creek was a cornucopia of so many living things. In early spring crabs crawled out of their holes, leaving behind pieces of mud, like sawdust, around the edges of the holes. We found the crabs in the shallows of the creek, around the riffles. A riffle is a narrow neck of the creek where the clear sparkling water runs swiftly with a gurgling sound. One could say that a riffle is a miniature rapids, but no one spoke of rapids in our humble creek.

In the riffles, one could spot the red crabs among the small stones, their bee-bee eyes rolling, their long feelers moving like TV antennae. When spooked, a crab can shoot away backwards as quick as the flash of a fish. So one must approach a crab carefully. Do not scare it. A crab will defend itself with its pincers claws. With thumb and forefinger poised, one grabs the crab by its bullet-like body. Held aloft, the crab wiggles like a sprung spring, its pincers desperately trying to claw its attacker and its tail rolled up under its body like a coiled snake.

Of a spring day, we found as many as ten or a dozen crabs, some six inches in length. We took them home, ruthlessly pulled off the claws and the tails and then roasted them over the blue flame of our natural gas range. The tails were the best. Each offered several good bites of white chewy meat, the texture of coconut, but the flavor of buttered chestnuts. We stuck a fork in the thin end of each claw and held it over the flame. The claw sizzled and sang and whistled like Aunt Annie's tea kettle. Then we cracked open the bright red claw and scratched out the white stringy meat. It, too, had the flavor of buttered chestnuts.

We made seines out of burlap gunny sacks, tying the four ends to two five-foot sticks. Or two larger kids simply took the gunny sack at its four corners and scooped through the water of the creek, holding the lower ends to the sand/mud bottom.

We seined the deeper water holes in the creek for minnows and craw dads. A craw dad is a miniature crab, yellowish gray in color, numerous only during a few weeks at the end of May and first part of June. Minnows were bait for crappies; craw dad tails were bait for catfish. A whole craw dad could bag you a nice sized bass.

Then once in a while the suckers would run. It took a certain combination of rains, warm weather, the height of the water in the creek to have the suckers come up from Grand Lake all the way to our part of the country. Spawning suckers ran the riffles at night.

So sucker hunting was a night expedition, with lanterns and flashlights. We went downstream as far as Ashman's thick woods. It was a wet, cold, sloppy time, with lots of shouting. There goes a big one! You missed him! We come home with a bucket full. Though suckers have the small bones of carp, their flavor early in the spring is fresh and pure. We ate them with great gusto, everyone trying to recognize the very fish that he or she captured.

Trapping season opened in late fall, early winter. The creek was home to muskrats. We trapped them with metal jump traps. Muskrats are rodents; they can be destructive to crops. Over the years, there seemed to have been a healthy ecological balance; there was no danger to the species and, at the same time, they did not become a major pest.

Later, Ohio changed its trapping laws. I do not want to become polemic or defend society ladies wearing natural fur coats. But farming families understand that life is give-and-take at all levels. Of course, muskrats must die for us to sell their pelts. Of course, occasionally we would come upon a trap snapped shut with a leg in it: a muskrat chewed off its own leg to escape. And sometimes we caught the same muskrat with only three feet.

Life is tough. We knew personally the steers which were slaughtered to put meat on our table. A superficial sentimentalism over animal rights is neither realistic nor good ecology.

Extra spending money was one motivation for trapping. But mostly, trapping was an adventure for us boys. On wet foggy nights the muskrats would come out early and we ran the traps at night.

There was nothing quite like the experience of checking a muskrat hole underneath the water level at night, especially if you were alone. You needed two hands. So you'd put the flashlight in your mouth, lie down on your stomach, run your hands from the wooden stake along the chain and carefully feel your way to the back of the trap to check if it was still set. Now if you came upon a live prey, it was some battle to subdue it, but carefully, in order not to mar the glossy, soft, brown fur.

Or the other experience. It is a cold morning. There is a cover of ice over the water. You are on your stomach, you break a hole through the ice, take off your gloves and your hands inch up to the trap. But you overreach, your stiffened fingers do not respond well and the trap snaps shut upon your fingers.

There is nothing to do but open the trap with the second hand. Then carefully, carefully, reset the trap and place it again in the entrance to the muskrat burrow. You pull away from the water, stagger to your feet, warm the aching fingers in your mouth and slowly take them out and try to pull on the gloves again. Without becoming macho about it, I claim this will make a man out of you.

The creek is still there. Red-wing black birds chirp in the willow rushes. There is that valiant flow of water. I take notice on my visits home that our friends, the muskrats, survive very well. I see occasional minnows and small fish.

But those wonderful red crabs and the masses of squirming craw dads have long disappeared, victims of detergents and chemicals. Our waterways have become depositories of chemicals and human and animal wastes in such quantities that they are hardly more than flowing cesspools. Why is there such an outcry against the trapping of fur-bearing animals and such indifference over other crimes against our common environment?

4.
Church Bells

From our front lawn you look to the southeast, and behind the cane press you see Nativity of Mary Church. It is of a gray stuccoed stone construction and, of course, like most of the churches of the area, it has a single high spire. Housed within the very top of the church steeple are two bells, one larger and one smaller. I am sure at the time the bells were blessed, each was given a "baptismal" name. The sound of ringing church bells made up an important part of our lives.

The bells rang the Angelus at six in the morning, at twelve noon and at six in the evening. Part of the School Teacher's contract was that he—yes, in the case of Cassella, it was always a man—would be church janitor, responsible for the maintenance of the church, heating in winter and the ringing of the bells. Of course, people criticized Teacher Eifert for not always being on time, expecting the accuracy of Big Ben in London. But can you imagine a schedule that included your personal attention at these three precise moments every day of the year and ringing for all the Masses and devotions on Sundays and Holy Days? On Sundays, there was an hour bell before every Mass, then a half hour bell, then the starting bell. Each ringing had its own style and rhythm.

The first time I saw the famous painting "The Angelus" of a peasant couple praying with bowed head as dusk falls over the countryside, I almost repeated the prayer in my heart. As family, we prayed the Angelus before meals and not in union with the ringing of the church bells. But so much of the day centered around hearing those three short dongs, repeated three times and then like an Alleluia chorus, the big bell sounded out the concluding prayer. Indeed, our whole world was thus transformed with the announcement that "the Word dwelt among us."

On our farm we heard the church bells from a distance. For us to be in town so near to the church when the bells rang out was a deafening, thrilling experience. The transition from horses to tractors had the unpredictable result that the drivers of tractors could not tell the hour by the ringing of the church bells.

When I served the peasant villages in the Central Andes of Peru, instantly I understood the meaning of church bells. Of course, the peasants had no timepieces, no watches, no clocks. The ringing of the first bell means (like the hour bell in Cassella): "Take notice!" The second ringing: "Get yourself ready." The third ringing: "It's serious. The priest is here. Mass is about to begin." I felt right at home.

The very word CASSELLA has its history. Linguists might think that it comes from the Italian and means "a little house." But there is little or no Italian presence in southern Mercer County, Ohio. CASSELLA, so goes the story, comes from the German word KAPPELLE, which means "chapel" or "church." For its first years, the settlement around the church was referred to simply as KAPPELLE. When the authorities in the state capitol, Columbus, Ohio, asked the residents the name of their town, they responded in German script: KAPPELLE. The Anglos in Columbus misread the letters and made the p's into s's. They wrote the name CASSELLA and the name has remained. So while there are places like Saint Henry, Saint Sebastian, Saint John, Saint Rose, we have the name Cassella.

The English poet John Donne writes;
"Send not to know
for whom the bell tolls;
it tolls for thee."

Again, with strong sentiments, I immediately recognized the intent of the lines. When a parishioner died, the news was conveyed to Teacher Eifert and he rang the church bells. It had its code. First, a prolonged heavy ringing. This meant: take notice: there has been a death. Then the slow tolling began, a ring for every year of the life of the deceased.

If we knew an aging neighbor had been very sick, we patiently counted out the years and simply prayed for the eternal rest of his/her soul. But if the church bells rang out when we knew of no one gravely ill: What has happened? Who died? And if the tolling stopped early, say, at thirty or forty gongs, who might it be that died at such an early age? Mom would discover that she needed Fleischmann's yeast or some bologna meat and would send a bigger kid to town to buy groceries, yes, but to find out who died and how.

The poet says: "It tolls for thee."

Yes, in a closely knit community, with a deep respect for life and death, each of us died a little with the death of a neighbor. We felt somehow that the bells were anticipating our own passing.

But the feeling is not one of despair or of undiluted sadness. The ringing of church bells is always a reassuring sign of a living community, a community of faith and hope. Church bells mean the abiding loving presence of God.

5.
Our Log House

When our Great Grandfather and our Great Grandmother with their four children arrived at Cassella on the feast of Corpus Christi, 1857, the area had been settled for over twenty years. Grandma died within a few months of arrival; Grandpa died some fourteen months later. Their death records and their tombstone (in German) are among the oldest in the parish. I visit their grave with awe and admiration.

Their oldest son, Christoph, our Grandfather, was twenty years old. He was about to be inducted into the Prussian army. The family was dirt poor, living off a few parcels of land in the village of Weinsheim on the small stream Nahe, which flows into the Rhine River below Mainz. Our Aunt Cora remembered many of her father's stories about life in Germany. One of them had it that, through a long winter, the only milk cow had nothing to eat. The family was forced to empty the straw from their sleeping mattresses so that the cow could survive—until spring.

Christoph announced he was going to America. The parents said: "If you go, the whole family goes." The mother was 59; the father, 60 years of age. They packed up what they could and boarded a ship at the town of Bingen, went down the Rhine, to England, to New York, across the Alleghenys to the Ohio River and up to Mercer County from Cincinnati. And there both parents were buried in less than two years.

Christoph Ranly married Elizabeth Bolley, moved into the Bolley family home, fathered three children from her and then had seven grown children from his second wife, Anna Marie Dietrich. The house and the land have stayed with the Ranly family ever since.

For all the glory we take in our log house, we feel a little sheepish about admitting that the Ranlys were not the original pioneers on the land and that our log house was not built by the Ranlys. We do not know the exact date of the log house. I calculate that it was most probably built in the early 1840's, on a high hill, to avoid the swampy marsh land of the primitive forests. So the house was probably some fifteen years old before Christoph Ranly came courting Elizabeth Bolley.

The Bolley house was a log house with two rooms and two rooms on the second floor. (I never figured out how the people got to the second floor in the original construction.) Later two rooms were added to the west, our kitchen and our sitting room. From the sitting room, stairs lead to the second floor bedrooms. Finally, a porch was added across the front; half of the porch was closed into what we called the porch room. The other half was open, which we called the front porch.

The doorway from the kitchen to Mom and Dad's bedroom and the doorway from the sitting room to the front room were cut through the original log structure. That means that these interior doorways are some two feet wide. Of course, the logs are covered with interior finished woodwork or plaster so that most people never notice anything strange. But all the original logs are still there, firmly in place, with the mortar (mud-mixed-with-straw) slapped in between the logs. In a recent redecorating of the family room my sister Rita threatened to expose the logs and create an interior decor around the natural logs. But the family was dead-set against the idea.

In time, even the two upstairs bedrooms were paneled. But in our day we slept next to the bare logs, worn smooth and shiny over the years. The mud mortar had been replaced with cement.

The logs are best seen from the cellar where huge logs make up the ceiling/roof. Our pioneers built sturdy homes. Aunt Angie lived in a little frame house in Fort Recovery. She used to tell us: "You do not have to worry about a wind storm in your house. You will see my house fly by in the wind and this house will still be as solid as a rock."

By our day a tin roof covered the original shingles. Night rains were welcome as the roof sang and danced to the rhythmic fall of rain drops. The one chimney served for the gas range in the kitchen and the wood burning stove in the sitting room. If we needed to heat the front room in winter, we opened the door from the sitting room and fired up the stove until the heat circulated into the front room. Later, we had a kerosene burner in the front room, which worked well enough when it did not smoke.

The Rita and Ray Flaute family has lived in our log house for almost fifty years. Their eight grown children (all have flown the coop by now) have their own memories, their own stories. That generation and now their children have many spook stories about ghosts, friendly ghosts, mysterious noises, strange goings on. I don't remember serious ghost stories in our time.

Oh, we have our own stories. For example: We kids are home alone. We are in the kitchen and in the sitting room. (No one, but no one was ever allowed in the front room, where the piano stood.) But did you hear that? Someone hit the piano keys! Who? There, again! How? Unmistakable. Some one is hitting the piano keys! YOU go see! No, YOU! There it goes again! Then it stops. Then from inside the front room comes a loud "Meow!" We open the door. Out steps Pet, our favorite mother cat. She had walked across the open keyboard of the piano.

Rita and Ray have a good sense of the value of history. They now serve as guides and caretakers of the Mercer County Historical Museum in Celina. The Flaute home, our log house, is a veritable museum in itself. There are framed collections of Indian arrowheads, spinning wheels, hand corn-planters, red walnut cupboards. Step in to visit them some day. Rita will invite you in and take you upstairs. In the middle upstairs room the original logs are exposed, with the natural wood and the natural mud mortar.

Who were the people who cut these trees? How did they select the trees, trim them, haul them here, place them, one on top of another? Who packed in this mud mortar?

Our log house deserves to have its many ghosts. But the best thing about our log house is that it is still home to us. We the living are its only ghosts.

6.
Summer

For us, summer began on Ascension Thursday, when we went fishing all day after the early Mass; summer ended, symbolically, on August 15, the Feast of the Assumption, when we went to the Mercer County Fair. I am sure that those responsible for the civic and liturgical calendars did not have the Ranly family in mind. We had no sense of the separation of Church and State. We learned how to integrate the passing seasons, the civic calendar and the practice of our Faith into a single, simple whole.

School was over well before Decoration Day, which was always on May 30 and not simply transferred to a weekend. May 30 is also my sister Ella Mae's birthday. On this day, in 1942, the gray mare foaled a beautiful spotted colt we called Pearl (in honor of Pearl Harbor). To this day, on May 30, in front of Ella Mae, we sing happy birthday to Pearl, the colt.

Summer was full of work, from simple gardening, mowing lawns with a long wooden-handled push mower, to the hard work of making hay, shocking grain and putting up new fences. And threshing, which is a story, a culture, all to itself. But we had our family games, watched the Cassella Owls play baseball on Sunday afternoons and took occasional trips, say, to Cincinnati to visit our sister, Sister Teresa, and then take in the City Zoo.

Dad's birthday was July 3 which was included into our Fourth of July. We could buy all the paper caps we wanted which made a little pop in our cap guns. When we scratched the caps open, one by one, they burned our right thumb nails a black-blue color. They made a dull plop and there was that sweet, acrid smell of the gray smoke, like gun powder. For us, fire crackers were few and far between. But we got carbite from Martin Feltz, the town blacksmith, and made our own explosions.

A quart paint can was the best. It was made of solid heavy tin and the lid fit tight. Make a hole in the bottom of the can. Put in a good pinch of white carbite and dampen it with spit or water. It begins to fizzle and give off gas. Secure the lid well. Wait a few seconds. With shoes on, step on the tin can and put a burning match to the hole at the bottom. There is an explosion equal to a good sized fire cracker. The lid goes flying. What excitement! Recover the lid. A new pinch of carbite, water, close the lid, listen for the fizzle, light a match. Bang! Our neighbors could not say that the Ranlys do not celebrate Independence Day!

Summer is homemade ice cream. Perhaps it was well planned, like on the Fourth of July. But on a regular hot Sunday afternoon, perhaps with company, the suggestion would be made: ice cream. Some men drove to St. Henry and brought home a cake of blue-white ice about a foot square. Mom and the girls began making the ice cream mix. The ice was split into a few large pieces and slipped into a tough gunny sack. Then someone broke up the ice into small pieces, slamming the sack with the sides of an axe cautiously, so that the sack was not cut open, but carefully, so that all the ice was about the size of large cubes.

Someone hauled up the wooden ice cream bucket freezer from the cellar where the dampness kept the bucket water tight. Ours made two gallons of ice cream. The women came with the ice cream mixture and the milk. It was poured into the tall, round heavy steel cylinder jar. The wooden beaters were inserted. The gears were meshed together and the top secured.

Then the cracked ice was scooped from the gunny sack and packed all around the inner cylinder. Mom supervised, scattering quantities of salt over the ice. The ice came to cover the whole gear mechanism and the empty gunny sack was put over the top.

Now came the task of turning the ice cream freezer. One of us turned the circular handle, about the size of a tire wrench. There were many opinions about a proper technique in turning ice cream. Some said, turn slow and regular, with a set, steady rhythm. Others said, turn fast; it freezes faster and the ice cream is more fluffy. In any case, turning the freezer took about twenty minutes. The cranking became harder, because the ice cream now was thicker. Some people wanted to add some last minute very fast turns to fluff up the contents. Finally, the ice cream was pronounced ready.

Mom and the girls returned with large spoons and bowls. Very carefully, the top cloth and the ice/salt had to be removed from the top of the freezer so that no salt would seep into the ice cream. The top was removed. There were awes of wonder and approval. It had been turned just right. Mom worked free the inner beater with its wooden sides and pulled it out carefully. But not too carefully! Because she would hand the beater to us kids and we licked it clean with spoons and with our tongues.

Immediately, the women began dishing out the newly made ice cream. We ate the first bowl in the purity of its vanilla flavor. Later, perhaps there were fresh strawberries or peaches or even a chocolate syrup. For us, the absolute best dish in the world, the very joys of heaven are summed up in one phrase: peaches and ice cream.

One eats homemade ice cream slowly. The cold can affect the sinuses and cause a real pain through the roof of the mouth and through the top of the nasal cavities. Some years later I came upon Ella Mae with a baby crying hard in her arms. I told her I would turn her in for cruelty to children. She explained the dilemma. The baby wanted ice cream but he ate it so fast his mouth hurt. He was unable to understand that what tasted so good was what caused all the pain. Maybe that's a summary of life itself. What feels so good is what causes so much pain.

Summer is wiener roasts. Yes, we called the meat stuck on pointed willow sticks and roasted over an open fire WIENERS and not hot dogs. Wiener roasts were more for youth, with town kids, after a Joe Louis prize fight. Wiener roasts in those days were not things that Mom and Dad planned and did with us as family.

We learned to let white fluffy marshmallows catch fire and glow like a gas mantle with an orange flame. Then blow out the flame and eat the black ashes along with all the gooey hot white insides in one big mouthful.

The generation after us made much more of families gathering around an early evening camp fire. Later began the tradition of the annual family camporee but that has its own history.

Summer is the County Fair. Our annual day at the fair was on August 15, which, as I said, was the Holy Day of the Assumption. We went to the fair after 10 a.m. church.

There are many romantic stories about county fairs: novels, movies, and so on. My older brothers and sisters had great experiences at the fair. I think my nephews and nieces celebrated and participated in the fair even more than the older generation. But I, myself, have very little to say about the fair as such. Some of my key years were the War years and the fair suffered. I was in the Four H Club only one or two years. I never exhibited animals at the fair, only potatoes one year. Oh, I enjoyed the midway, the exhibition booths, the animal barns, the trotting racing horses. We ate hokey-pokey ice cream. Once I got sick to the stomach on the ferris wheel. But the fair became a symbolic thing. It meant the end of summer.

The tomatoes were now ripe. Melons began to turn yellow and orange. The pickle patch was running out. The mornings had a new crispness to the air. Mom took us to Penny's and groused about how much our feet grew going barefoot all summer. Now what sized shoes must we have for school? Bats would come flying out from the cedar trees in the orchard and sweep low over the barnyard. Owls would screech after sundown. No more sleeping on the front lawn on those unbearably hot nights. The fresh wheat straw in the bottom mattress would crunch as we fought over the first thin blanket of the season.

Summer was passing.

7.
Hay Making

Before the Fourth of July we already had put away the first cutting of hay. By my time, we had very little timothy or red clover; it was mostly alfalfa. In good summers we could get three cuttings. The first was the biggest and the most important. The phrase, make hay while the sun shines, meant just that. Get the hay into the barn as soon and as fast as possible. Prolonged rains on cut hay could spoil the hay.

What combines did to threshing, what corn pickers did to the corn shredder, the field hay bailer did to hay making. We never had silos. My account is of the pre-hay bailer era, when hay making was an all-family job.

A horse-drawn hay mower left the green hay cut and lying flat. The hay needed two to three days of hot sun and dry wind to dry. Our first hay rake was a simple tool with a rack of rounded tines in back. The operator rode on an uncomfortable steel seat and controlled a long wooden handle which would lift up the back fork. He drove the horse (or mule, in the early days) over the dry hay and lifted the fork where he wanted to make a windrow. The whole operation was manual and often the results showed a lot of human error. Some patches of cut hay lay untouched; the windrows were very uneven.

The second hay rake was the side deliverer, a much more complicated and efficient piece of machinery which nicely rolled the hay into long, straight windrows. More or less, with the first hay rake, we pitched hay by hand. By the time of the side deliverer, we had a hay loader.

In both cases, packing the hay wagon took skill; it became an art. If men pitched the hay, forkful by forkful, one could control the packing rather easily. But with a hay loader picking up the windrows and dropping the hay upon the wagon in a steady, dusty stream, the two packers on the wagon were kept very busy. One had to lay a good foundation with the loose hay. Then build up the two sides, fill in the middle, keep checking to see that the load is rising straight. A lopsided load might tip before it got to the barn. But it was primarily a case of pride and aesthetics. A well-built load of loose hay was a piece of beauty and its creators deservedly felt proud of their work.

One drove the team of horses with the load of hay up to the unloading area with great care. For one thing, the driver sat at the very top of the load; the long reins were stretched to their last inch. The driver must set the wagon as close to the barn as possible. It was like driving a car over the track of a garage pit.

Putting loose hay in the hay mow of the barn involved the coordination of many elements. I remember hay making in the old barn, but here I will describe the operation in the new barn. In the old barn, the wagon was unloaded from inside the barn, from the threshing floor. With the new barn, the hay was unloaded from one or the other of the two ends of the barn, outside. Our barn is in the Mercer County Book of Big Barns as one of the very few barns with two gables, which allowed unloading hay from both ends. Mostly, we unloaded the hay from the north side of the barn, where Mom could watch the proceeding from the house.

It was basically a simple case of ropes and pulleys. Start from the top of a wagon loaded with hay. You have in your hands a large hay fork which you insert into the loose hay. You set the fork so that it can lift up a good-sized load of hay. The fork is attached to a strong twine rope. The rope comes directly from a pulley overhead; in our case, this pulley is at the far outer end of the roof gable extended out from the barn, like a bill on a baseball cap.

Now the rope is threaded through another pulley at the far end of the barn. From there it drops to the floor of the barn, where another pulley guides the rope out the side door to the corner of the wind pump. There the last pulley directs the rope to the doubletree, where the team of horses is hitched (the same horses that pulled the wagon in from the field). From the hay wagon the man shouts: "Ready!" when he has the hay fork firmly stuck into the loose hay.

The one driving the horses urges them forward with a "Giddap!" The rope draws taut from pulley to pulley. The horses lean into the pull. The forklift on the top of the wagon begins to tear away from the wagon a sizable clump of hay. Once freed from the wagon, the clump of hay attached to the fork swings and sways, but it rises steadily with the force and the speed of the horses pulling below.

At the very top of the barn gable and all along the very inside tip of the roof there is a bolted iron track, like a single suspended railroad track. Outside, under the gable, at the very tip, there is a carrier on this track. When the fork is pulled into the carrier, it trips a switch and the carrier slides across the track into the barn. The man on the top of the hay wagon is watching all this with two ropes in his hands. Inside the hay mow some one shouts: "Now!" The wagon man pulls the trip rope. The fork opens and the clump of hay falls loose inside the hay mow with a loud thud and a thick cloud of dust.

The horses stop and are turned around. The big rope is dragged back to the nearest pulley by the wind pump. The man on the wagon pulls the second small rope. This brings the empty carrier back to the end of the barn where it releases the fork which drops gently down onto the top of the hay wagon. Now one must study how to insert the fork for a second load.

And so it goes. It takes six or seven or eight fork loads to unload an ordinary wagon of hay.

As a small boy, what am I doing? Unloading loose hay involves the coordination of a closely knit team of workers. My job is pulling rope. That is to say, when the horses come to the end of their pull, the driver unhitches the doubletree from the rope and drives the team back to their starting point. This leaves the rope stretched out along the whole length of the barnyard. Now the man on the hay wagon must pull hard on the second rope to bring the fork back down to the wagon. I must pull the rope lying loose on the ground and bring it back and ease it into the pulley by the wind pump so that the wagon man can pull the fork back with less difficulty.

While he sets the fork for a new lift of hay, the driver couples the horses to the rope again. "Ready!" The rope becomes taut, the new load lifts free of the wagon. It hits the track and slides down the track inside the barn. Someone from the hay mow shouts: "Now! Okay!" The hay falls with a cloud of dust.

A few years later when I am older, I am working in the hay mow, scattering the hay, tearing it away from those fallen clumps in the middle. We want the hay loose. It will dry better. It will be easier to take out next winter, when we must drop the loose hay down the chutes to feed the horses and the cows.

Working in the hay mow is hot and dusty. It is the most disagreeable task in making hay.

Someone has to do it.

8.
Dad

Dad was forty-two when I was born in 1930, so when I was old enough to remember him, he was in his late forties. Only recently did I do the mathematics. I remember Dad as old man. But now when I am approaching the age at which Dad died I am aghast and feel guilty that I cannot remember him as being a young man, say, as I think of myself as young at 50.

Years ago, someone in the family—I think it was Father Vic—reproduced and magnified and touched up a small black and white photo of Dad when he was twenty-some. He sports a thin mustache, has his shirt collar open over a suit coat and has a smart glint in his eyes. I have always had this photo with me in my many years in Peru.

Dad kept all of us housed and fed and clothed by farming eighty-six acres of rather poor Ohio farmland. For years, he rented land from neighbors to the east and to the west. But as Mom often said, Dad was never cut out to be a farmer. His genes made him a near genius in so many other fields.

Dad was a musician. His principal instrument was the fiddle: not the violin, the fiddle. A fiddle is to a violin what the bush leagues are to professional baseball. A fiddler is all heart, sincerity, dedication, who plays for the fun of the game.

Dad played fiddle for the Pete Studer Band. The group was popular for barn dances, wedding dances or a good neighborhood romp. He read music well and gave lessons not only on the violin, but also on the cello, the trombone, the trumpet and the tuba bass.

We have pictures of Dad as a young man playing in the Cassella band.

He sang first tenor in the men's church choir. For the early dawn Mass on Christmas, Dad played Silent Night on the violin from the choir loft in the back of church

Music was always part of the family. Alvina, the oldest, knew piano well enough to play with Dad in Pete Studor's Band. We always had a secondhand upright piano in the front room.

For years, it was a roller player piano. There was a number of paper rolls stored below the top of the piano stool. The rolls were punched full of little programmed holes and the roll was carefully inserted into the head of the piano. Then by pumping two foot pedals, like organ pedals, "I'm Forever Blowing Bubbles" came flowing through the piano keys. Many rolls had words to the songs scripted on the side so we would sing along with great gusto. Now in bars they do the same thing with screens and loud speakers and call it karaoke or something like that.

What was real fun was trying to fool company. By pushing a button, the piano keys could be turned off or on. So one could sit on the piano stool, pump the air pumps and run his/her hands over the keyboard with great aplomb. Visitors would be most impressed and even applaud such a virtuoso performance.

But all of this is an aside. I was talking about Dad.

For several decades, Dad was president of the School Board. This allowed him various privileges. For example, the president had the right to a large, light-colored wooden rolltop desk. This desk became a mainstay in the front room. When Dad finally gave up the presidency, they took away the rolltop desk. Then we bought a small, wooden, dark brown desk that just never did for us what the rolltop did.

Another privilege was a bit rare. Once a year a "honey dipper" cleaned out the two outside toilets on the school grounds. The president of the School Board had the right to have the contents dumped as enriched fertilizer on his own land. Dad would pick a particularly barren hillside. The "honey dipper" came up the lane with a few barrels on his horse-drawn cart and spread the contents over the indicated hillside. It was a marvel how the crops would be extra green and verdant and productive on that small piece of land. Ah, sweet mystery of life!

For years, Dad was County Assessor. He worked at this from January through March, until the spring farm work began. When President Roosevelt tried to control the over-marketing of agricultural products, Dad had the job of measuring the size of farmers' plantings.

I helped him with this. We had a wire tape measure a hundred feet long which rolled up into a figure eight. We had a number of wire stakes. Dad gave me one end of the tape measure and then he would walk off with the rest of the tape measure. When he came to the end of the hundred feet we stretched the measure taut. At that point, he stuck a wire stake in the ground. Then he motioned me to follow him. We walked in a straight line until I came upon the wire stake. We both would stop, stretch out the wire measure and Dad would put down a new stake. I would pick up the one left behind. As we came to the end of the field we would carefully check the exact feet on the measure. Then I would produce the number of wire stakes I had recovered. For example, five stakes meant five hundred feet, plus whatever the last measurement showed. We measured the two sides of a rectangular field and then calculated its exact acreage. It was simple, fundamental and quite exact.

I was so impressed by the great number of people Dad knew as friends and by the great respect the people showed Dad.

Dad knew how to repair shoes, putting on new soles, sewing up the backs.

Dad knew how the gas well worked at the cane press; he helped the Feltz boys clean the well once a year.

Dad kept bees.

Every election day Dad served on the Election Board at the C.K. of A. Hall in Cassella.

Dad tended bar at the Dahlinghaus saloon on Sunday afternoons.

Dad was top supervisor of a threshing rig for over thirty years.

Like an architect and civil engineer Dad supervised the building of the new barn.

Children always look upon their fathers as almighty God-figures. For us, there seemed to be good reasons for our respect for Dad.

Dad was not the cuddly, sentimental father-knows-best type we came to know on TV serials. He was the boss; we knew that. But he was not authoritarian or picky or arbitrary in his demand for discipline and order.

In and outside our home there was only one code: honesty, fair play and straight talk. Punishment in school was seconded by hard talk and possible punishment at home. The authority and the right of the Teacher were never questioned before us children.

We tried to resolve the many differences among ourselves without recourse to Mom or Dad. Or else, we took our problems to Mom, because if a scrap between us kids ever got appealed to the highest authority in the house—to Dad—then even the winner would lose. So, of course, we often used Mom to plead our cases before Dad. We watched the action between them with great reserve and expectation.

Dad and Mom (and the older children) spoke German as their first language. We youngsters used German only in a few funny expressions, to count or to cuss. We could not follow or participate in a German conversation. So in our presence, if Dad and Mom wanted to converse in private, they switched to German. This was how many of our requests to Mom were resolved with Dad. Topics like Santa Claus and Easter Eggs could be discussed at the supper table in front of us young kids and we sat dumbfounded because the conversation was in German. We suspected some kind of shenanigans was going on but we did not know what.

In this context, the whole family was eating supper in our hot and crowded kitchen on a day in late August, 1944. It was my last meal before leaving on the morrow by train from Van Wert to go to Brunnerdale Seminary, Canton, Ohio. It was not a really big farewell dinner, but we were all conscious that this was a special moment.

At the time, four of our brothers were in the Armed Forces: three in the Pacific Area, in active conflict. Could Dad afford to let another fourteen-year-old son leave the farm? He answered: If the government can take four of my boys, I guess I can give one more to God.

As I said, the meal was not all that solemn. That was not our style. But

44

then Mom spoke up in her loving, humorous, but very insightful way. "Ach," she said, "Ernie will get homesick and in three days he'll come back home."

At that, Dad laid down his fork and knife and spoke directly to me. Mom sat at the head of the table near the gas range. Dad sat to her left. We kids all sat on a long bench along the wall. Dad looked at me across the table. "You will stay three or four months. You will try out the life. Then in three months, if you want to come home, that will be all right. But not before you give it a try of three months." Solomon had spoken.

Divine Providence dealt Dad a bad hand of cards. At a relatively early age, Dad suffered a series of strokes, leaving him always a little weaker, less independent. Mom (and all the rest at home) nursed him along. Dad played the hand dealt to him as well as he could.

By the time of my priestly ordination I sensed that Dad felt left out of much of the preparation going on. So I asked him to write in longhand a commemorative verse on the back of some of my memorial cards. This Dad did with a shaky but legible hand.

I don't know how many of these cards have been preserved among family and relatives. I know I cherish the few I have.

9.
The Summer Kitchen

It was called the summer kitchen. The idea was that during the heat of summer, cooking over a wood fire and eating in the house were too hot. So families cooked and ate in the summer kitchen. Of course, the family ate in the kitchen. I don't think we knew what a dining room was—or a dining area, as they say about today's new houses. Some still call a large family kitchen a "farmer's kitchen."

I never knew our summer kitchen to function as a kitchen. For one reason, we had natural gas, so summer cooking—while bad—was not all that hot. Also, the kitchen was on the northwest side of the house so the direct sun hit it only in late afternoon. Before anyone even dreamt of air conditioning, one accepted the fact that summertime was hot.

Then there was the smoke house. Yes, I do remember well how Dad used hickory chips to smoke pork hams, sausages and ribs in the smoke house. The clapboard white building had a small overhanging roof where there hung a large dinner bell. We never actually rang the bell for dinner.

Behind the smoke house there was what people in nice society call the outhouse, but which we simply called the toilet, a two-holer, with a stock of old catalogues. All the functions that went on there were simply referred to as "going to the toilet." Nothing was more simple and more natural.

The room attached to the summer kitchen (later it became the woodshed) still had brick ovens and a brick floor, but I never knew the time when the ovens were actually used to bake bread.

The whole space between the back porch, the summer kitchen and the smoke house was paved with blue-gray rocks, about the size of softballs, which had been carefully selected from the creek bed and laid with great care and precision.

In 1989 when Rita stepped into the courtyard of the Ranly ancestral house in Weinsheim, Germany, she cried out: "Paving stones! Just like home!" And so it was.

Emigrants leave home with a lot of baggage. They then find ways of reconstructing their own past in new settings. A simple thing: hand picked rocks to make a paved inner yard. It was Weinsheim, Germany, transplanted to Cassella, Ohio, in the last half of the nineteenth century.

The summer kitchen was the center of activity on butchering days. Then its wood-burning stove, its tables, its brick floor gave a kind of professional setting to all the carefully programmed activity of butchering. But the excitement and the thrill of butchering is a story in itself.

February 22 is George Washington's birthday (as well as the birthday of our oldest sister, Alvina). The exact day was always a holiday, a day free from school, free from classes. A fire was built in the summer kitchen stove and we spent the day shelling seed corn.

That is to say, during fall corn husking, Dad—and the older brothers—carefully selected and set aside the best looking ears of corn, those with long, straight rolls of bright yellow kernels. These were hung to dry in the granary, hanging from their own husks. Then on George Washington's Birthday we would sit on wooden benches around the wood-burning stove and carefully shell the corn—break off the kernels from the cob into a tin pan or bucket. To avoid blisters (which were common and painful) one learned to use a smaller corn cob as a kind of rasp under the right hand.

Within the few bushels of yellow field corn there were always a few very carefully selected ears of red corn. In the spring planting, there would be one red seed kernel to perhaps every 200 or 300 yellow kernels. Then in the fall husking, it would be a great surprise and a reward to shuck out an ear of red corn.

Actually, among all the regular yellow ears, one could spot a red one by the color and texture of its silk and its husk. So at times there would be a tussle between us to grab the red corn stalk away from the person sitting opposite as we went through, stalk by stalk, a shock of corn now lying on the ground. That red ear of corn, thrown upon the growing pile of yellow corn, was like a star on a Christmas tree. A real prize, a jewel.

Also, on George Washington's Birthday, we had to shell popcorn. We usually had the small white kerneled popcorn, which, while small, exploded into white crispy pieces of cotton, absolutely irresistible. Our family always ate all the popcorn in sight. There was never leftover popcorn.

Because George Washington's Birthday was a free day, Mom let us end the day playing cards or table games. We learned the rather complex game of pinochle by second or third grade. We played with a great competitive spirit: winner take all!

Mom enjoyed winning as much as any of us. Yet she was always big enough to find words of consolation for the losers. She would not tolerate excessive teasing, but the winners were allowed their time to gloat. Just wait till next time! Then Mom's last words of wisdom (which really were not a big consolation): Someone has to lose!

Over time, the summer kitchen simply did not live up to its name. So the men devised a plan to open up the whole south end and convert the space into a two-car garage. Up to that time, our '32 Plymouth was housed in the machine shed, beyond the hog stable. The brick floor disappeared (as did all the bricks from the wood stable) and the front of the garage had a work table and tool bench. Then later, this garage, in turn, was remodeled and expanded, so that most of the paving stones disappeared.

The concept of a summer kitchen was converted somehow into the outdoor grill. Now during the hot summer, people cook and eat outside. About which, Martin Feltz, the town blacksmith, made the comment: "We used to eat in the house and go to the toilet out back. Now we go to the toilet in the house and eat outside."

Well, being a blacksmith, he didn't really say "go to the toilet." There is a shorter, single word more expressive.

But who can hold back progress and proper society?

10.
Threshing

Heine Hierholzer owned the threshing rig where Dad worked summers for over thirty years. Threshing was a major part of our lives.

I must repeat here that this is my stuff: what I know and what I remember. Sharing threshing stories often results in widely divergent accounts.

For example, I do not remember steam engines. I've seen steam engines on exhibit at county fairs. But the tractor I remember was a Hoover tractor, immense, with iron wheels almost two feet wide, wheels eight feet tall. We watched that Hoover tractor come down the road from Ashman's hill, pulling the threshing machine slowly and steadily like some huge caterpillar, turning carefully into the lane and crossing the bridge to the trepidation of us kids.

Since our barn and cow yard were on a hill, Dad and the rest of the crew had the difficult task of getting the separator to sit at an even till. Heavy planks were placed under this wheel, under that wheel. Dad kept testing the lay with a small shining pocket level. One of Dad's lasting criticisms against the combine was that it could not possibly clean the grain efficiently because the separator units must be at a perfect level set.

Poor Dad. To him the combine was like a monster from outer space invading that secure little world of threshing rings. I was home on vacation one summer and observed how Dad, for the first time and out of necessity, had reluctantly hired a combine to harvest his grain. Threshing had gone the way of the horse and buggy.

In fact, threshing created and sustained a very large world; it was a society and a culture in itself.

The grain was cut when still somewhat green and sturdy to avoid the threat of destructive wind and rain in the last weeks of ripening. The grain binder was a mechanical marvel, with dozens of semi-independent but overlapping and coordinated operations. The cutting sickle worked like any hay mower. The wooden ferris wheel guided the cut grain on to the moving platform, a canvas conveyor belt, with its wooden slats, which carried the cut stalks of grain into the binding machinery.

The wonder of wonders was how the tyer worked, pulling string from a ball of twine, tying a secure knot around a sheaf of grain about ten inches in circumference and cutting off the twine. Then another action kicked the bundle out of the binder on to a cradle which dropped four or five bundles to the ground on one heap.

All of this worked from the power of one large drive wheel in the center of the binder. The wheel moved only by the force of pulling. I do not remember horses pulling a binder. By my day we had the old Fordson tractor and later that green monster, the John Deere D.

The first cutting around the field cut the grain nearest the fence row with the machinery tramping down the grain. The second round was in the opposite direction to pick up the trampled grain. Then the cutting went around and around, the area of standing grain always getting smaller.

We all invaded the field to shock the grain. We wore broad-rimmed straw hats for protection from the sun and long-sleeved shirts for protection from the scratchy straw and heads of grain. Wheat would be cut towards the end of June; oats, about the second week of July.

To shock grain, usually two people worked together. They synchronized their stomping, securing together the first two bundles into the stubbles and to the ground. This served as a kind of stump or base. Then ten or twelve bundles were set up in a tight circle around this center. The shock would be topped by taking a particularly large bundle, spreading open the grain heads and laying the bundle on the very top of the shock at a slight angle so that rain water would run off. The shocks were lined up in loosely ordered rows.

What a great sight to finish shocking wheat in the field by the barn, just at dusk, with the sun slipping behind the catalpa grove! The stubbles were cut very low because wheat straw was also a premium. The newly cut stubbles gleamed golden in the rays of the setting sun. The rows upon rows of shocks looked like the desert tents of the Israelites that we saw in our Bible history texts.

The threshing ring made its first round through our neighborhood threshing wheat; then it returned again several weeks later to thresh oats. Mom and the ladies-threshing neighbors worked like Santa's elves in the house.

Yet they had to watch closely what was going on outside. The latest report said that the threshing at Ashman's would be finished before noon but that all the hands would eat dinner there. That meant that the Pete Ranlys must serve afternoon lunch and late supper. Hopefully, rain would not delay the schedule.

A team of glistening red-brown horses came trotting up the lane, pulling the first flat hay wagon. (Our horses were a team of grays.) Every hand knew what to do.

Dad and the boys had made out the list the night before. So many wagons with two men on a wagon; so many in the field with their three-pronged pitch forks; so many to carry the sacks of grain to the granary. The number of men equaled the number of places and jobs that we Ranlys had worked with our neighbors. All was a gentleman's working agreement. No one worked for money; no one worked by the clock. This is what threshing neighbors was all about.

This year I was to be the water boy. I carried with me a one gallon glass jug, full of fresh drinking water. I brought water not only to the men tending to the threshing machine itself and to those carrying the sacks of grain to the granary. I also had to carry water to all the men in the fields.

A threshing hand motioned to me that he wanted a drink. I screwed off the metal lid from the gallon jug. The man took the jug, shook a few drops on the ground and then hoisted the jug to his mouth and drank long, deep draughts of water. The men would help throw the water jug up to the packers on a full wagon of grain. A good water boy added to the morale of the threshing hands.

Packing the wagon was a skill, similar to packing a hay wagon. The larger stubble ends of the sheaves were lined carefully on the outer sides of the wagon. Two men on the ground pitched the bundles onto the wagon in a soft arch. The packers placed each bundle in its very proper place. The man on the front of the wagon, who owned the rig, drove the horses. There was a rhythm to the work and a minimum of talking. To draw up to the threshing machine with a well-stacked load filled the packers with pride. To have a load overturn was a tremendous embarrassment.

The driver guided the team of horses up to the threshing machine, calming them in the face of all the noise and dust. He placed the wagon carefully, expertly alongside the open feeder. Heine Hierholzer sat on the Hoover tractor, spitting tobacco juice, controlling the speed of the large belt which ran off the power wheel of the tractor and which was the moving force behind all the operations of the separator.

With the wagon in place, the tractor was revved up to full power. Two men on top of the wagon began unloading the wagon, deftly picking up with a fork each sheaf of grain and tossing it on to the feeder belt, the grains forward. The sheaves disappeared under the revolving cutter blades.

Soon a rhythm set in between the two men on the wagon. Overloading the feeder would make it choke. One bundle from the front; one bundle from the back.One from the front, one from the back. The Hoover tractor, with its whirling belt, puffed and snorted. The sheaves disappeared into the shark-like teeth of the cutter. A series of pans with different sized screens shook the grains, separating them from the chaff. The bulky straw moved on into the mawl of the blower fan which sent it flying in wind and dust out of the blower.

The grain itself was conveyed off to the side where it fell from a steel pipe. The pipe had a double opening with clamps to hold two grain sacks. A man stood watching his own sack fill up with red, clean grains of wheat. With the sack full, he switched the lever and the wheat began to fall into the second sack. He stepped back, closed his hands around the top of the open sack, hoisted the sack to his shoulders and walked off to carry the grain to the designated granary. Five/six men formed the brigade to carry and dump the sacks of grain into the granary.

Now stretched out to its full length like a boom on a ship was the straw blower, belching straw and dust. The blower was a large tube, two feet in circumference and some fifteen feet long. In his day, Dad had the reputation of being an expert blower-tender, building straw stacks into perfectly rounded mountains which would withstand the coming year's rain, snow and wind.

On my last summer home I helped Dad a few days tending blower when one of the regular hands was sick. Dad and I sat together on a wooden plank on the very top of the rig. Dad carefully set the swing of the blower, while, with a thin rope, he controlled the open end where the straw came tumbling out in a yellow golden stream.

Laying the foundation for the straw stack was fundamental. Dad had to calculate how many wagon loads of grain this particular farmer's land would produce. If one made the foundation of the straw stack too small, when the extra straw came in, one must add a second, smaller stack, which was derisively called a "junior." But by February, this "junior" stack would slide off the major stack and be stomped into waste by the cows. A bad scene. If one made the foundation of the stack too large, there was not enough straw to top it off and the stack sunk and dropped in. This was called a "pancake." The winter snows and early spring rains would not run off and, again, the straw would rot in the stack. Also a bad scene.

So Dad, calculating, watchful, laid the foundation of the stack. Then he let me handle the rope which controlled the very nose of the blower. We were to build up the periphery of the growing mountain of a straw stack and only later, slowly, fill in the center.

Sitting on that shaking, convulsing machine with the wind-tunnel noise of the blower, I felt like the king of the cowboys, riding a bucking bronco in the best of Western movies.

When Dad saw the last wagons come in, he crawled up beside me and, without pushing me aside, directed the last fifteen minutes or so of the operation. This meant bringing the stack to a perfectly rounded top and blowing loose straw all up and down the stack to let fall a last layer of straw like powdered sugar upon a muffin.

Dad took his reputation very seriously. A good straw stack was recognized as a piece of art. It would be appreciated through the late spring of the next year if and when there was still standing a supply of clean dry straw for bedding down the cow stables.

Central to the mystique of the threshing culture were the meals. Family after family outdid themselves to serve hot, tasty, plentiful meals. Some families had distinctive specialties, such as cherry pies or pork sausage. The most common threshing meal was roast beef, mashed potatoes and gravy. Louie Strukamp got away with serving spare ribs and sauerkraut and since he was the only one who served such a common menu it was received with great enthusiasm.

On those few times that I worked with Dad on the threshing crew, I came up to the house, dusty and black like a ship's fireman. So with the other grown, grisly, working hands, I went to the washing area under a tree on the lawn. I filled a basin with cold water, set it on a wooden bench, took a bar of soap and, snorting and blowing through mouth and nose, I washed off the dust and dirt from face, neck, hair and hands. The towel was a cotton cloth, no cannon terry towel. After that, I ate with great gusto. The ladies served the men with smiling faces and offered serving after serving. But I ate only two pieces of cherry pie out of courtesy and respect.

Mr. Hierholzer always moved on with his rig on the same day. That small train/caterpillar—the Hoover tractor and the long, silver, glistening separator—crossed the bridge and moved down the lane as slowly as it came. We had little time to feel sad because there was cleaning up to do around the area where the threshing machine stood.

So now we had a new straw stack. It gave our farm a new identity for the next ten months. Now when we fell off walking the top board of the fence around the cowyard we fell on soft new straw.

When the cows were let in, they trampled into manure the straw around the bottom of the stack. The cows loved to rub their backs up against the straw. Soon there was a solid wall all around the base of the straw stack, the height of the cows. The straw hung over this circular walkway like a cloister roof. It was like a well-trimmed hedge, kept clean and trim simply by the action of the cows.

When fall and winter came along bedding was carried into the stables from the straw stack. By now, with the wind and rain and snow, the straw stack had settled down into a solid mass. Then we used the long handled straw hook, a piece of iron some four feet long, with a hooked barb at one end and a round handle at the other end.

You rammed the barbed point into the side of the straw stack (where the cows had rubbed it clean and bare), twisted the rod and pulled out a few tufts of straw. You did it again at the same spot. By the fifth or sixth pull, a good handful of loose straw would come out. With a pile of straw on the ground at your feet, you swooped it up in your open outstretched arms and, like carrying a basketful of dry wash clothes, you carried the straw into the barn and scattered it around the cow stables.

The straw stack was a permanent place of enchantment. If we needed twine strings we walked slowly around the stack to spot the twine within the straw and pull them out, one by one—the strings which the binder had so mysteriously tied together last summer. We would patiently dig tunnels into the very center of the stack and, like miners, carve little caverns and dark rooms inside. We needed a flashlight for illumination. Matches around the barn were totally forbidden.

There are those occasional bright cold days in the dead of winter. On the south side of the straw stack (if we got there before the cows) we would bury ourselves in the golden soft straw, soak in the rays of the sun, and forget about the foot of snow covering the straw stack above our heads.

Of course, the cows left their droppings all around, but we learned to live with reality and how to step around "cow pancakes" like one avoids water puddles in the rain. But if the truth be told, on a cold winter day, the steam and the smell coming off a recently laid cow pancake was not all that unpleasant.

The annual cycle of the threshing story would end only in April and May. The straw stack had finally disappeared, used up for bedding or trampled into manure in the cow yard itself. The oats now was sowed and one tested the ground every day to begin the spring ploughing. But first, the manure must be hauled.

The cow stables and horse stables had been cleaned out when necessary and convenient during the winter. Now for spring it was everything: all the manure must be put on the corn ground before ploughing. And everything meant the whole cowyard.

A manure fork has four prongs. It is not to be used like a spade. You slide it under the straw manure, pile it up into a little mound and then toss it on to the waiting manure spreader.

The famous mark of manure spreaders, New Idea, was invented and manufactured in our part of Ohio. It was our contribution to the industrialization and technification of farming until it, too, went the way of the horse and buggy.

Three/four of us boys could fill up a manure spreader rather rapidly. While it was taken out to the fields to have its contents spread over the future corn fields, we had a few minutes of time to play corn cob ball (a real Ranly family creation).

Spring is robins and early flowers and spawning fish. Spring is also spreading manure. Smell that sweet country air.

So when the cow yard is clean, the cows are let out to pasture day and night. The wheat now is in full head and the whole field is changing color from a dark green to a light yellow.

It is time that someone check the grain binder. It takes a good day to oil it, grease all the moving parts and double-check to see if all the chains and gears and sprockets are in working order.

Threshing season is almost here again.

11.
Mickey

Duke was the dog the older people talk about. I knew only one collie: Mickey. He was prettier and nicer than the full bred collies we saw in the movies, such as Lassie. Mickey had a shorter nose and was more plump, but he was unmistakably collie, with white and yellow markings and a long bushy tale.

Dad loved dogs. Mom learned to tolerate dogs. It was agreed that small dogs, like the terrier Tricksie or the 47-varieties Jenny, could come in the house but that big dogs had to stay outside. Huh! Mickey spent half of his life in the house.

We had three alarm systems. The first was the bridge with the rattle of its loose planks when a car crossed it. (The boys coming home late from dances and parties tried to cross the bridge without being heard. They seldom succeeded.) Then we had the flock of guinea fowl that slept in the cedar tree by the hog lane. The guineas slept lightly and created a great racket when something moved near them. The third alarm was a pair of dogs.

We never considered our dogs dangerous, but visitors approached them with great caution. For example, Mickey would bark rather disinterestedly at the milkman, until the man kicked at the little dog that was snapping at his pants leg. Then Mickey's upper lip would roll back and he would snarl like a monster in the movies. People learned to treat him with respect.

We kids at home could play with Mickey, roll with him over the grass, and have him return sticks or balls, although he was reluctant to drop the ball once he had it in his mouth.

Mickey performed one trick well. On command he would sit on his haunches and bark, one bark at a time, to the command: Speak!

We loved to trick other kids with the superior intellectual ability of Mickey, the dog. We would have him sit and then ask him very difficult mathematical problems. "Mickey. Speak! How much is forty divided by ten?" At the moment he barked four times he immediately won a caressing reward from us. The town kids were dumbfounded at his intelligence.

Dad's love for Mickey was returned by him a hundred-fold, although Dad teased him mercilessly. As is common with dogs, Mickey was very sensitive to music, to high sounds, even to the sound of a car horn. Coming home from Sunday Mass, Dad would open the front door of the car to pet Mickey on the head. Mickey would be there, tail wagging, all friendship and smiles. Then Dad would sound the horn. Poor Mickey would howl like a wolf baying at the moon. Or in the front room, Dad would play his fiddle like mad to get a rise out of Mickey. The two of them would put on a mad concert, like something out of a Marx Brothers movie. Yet the two of them were inseparable. How many black-and-white photos do we have with Dad and Mickey together!

Because Lucille lived and worked away from home so much she never became intimate with Mickey and never learned to trust him. We kids knew all of Mickey's moods and knew that he would never really hurt anyone. But Lucille was not sure. So if we got into a "fight," a good argument with Lucille, we called in Mickey.

Say, Ella Mae balked at wiping dishes after dinner and Lu would be scolding her. Mickey would come up with a half snarl and a bark and defend Ella Mae. Lucille felt intimidated. Ella Mae could calmly walk away. You learn how to play your cards.

Mickey's heavy coat of long hair made him suffer from summer heat. Listless, hunting for shade, he panted like a cow in heat. He found a spot on the south side of the house in front of the small cellar windows from which cool air escaped. Mom could never keep nice flowers in front of those cellar windows. If the front room was open, Mickey would lie in front of the small wooden cellar door because the crack by the floor allowed cool air to come out.

Mickey helped drive the cows to and from the pasture. Mickey was a scourge to any pig that broke out. Mickey was a good fighter. He took on many a ground hog, which are vicious rodents and killer-fighters. But Mickey always left a ground hog dead.

Robert Frost says that fences make good neighbors. In our area, hostile dogs made good neighbors. People did not want their dogs running pack with neighbors' dogs. We said that our dogs "should not loaf with neighbors' dogs."

Also, a dog should be a watch dog on its own turf and not be friendly to other dogs encroaching on its territory. So hostility between neighboring dogs was encouraged. When Mickey rolled and twisted in a really serious fight with Ashman's dog, we all looked on for some time. We were not overly concerned because we knew Mickey could hold his own. Eventually, the dogs were pulled apart and the neighbors in effect shook hands. With hostile dogs we all remained friends.

Dad and Mickey grew old together, Dad in his rocking chair in the sitting room, Mickey lying on the floor by his side. By this time I had left home and I cannot say who passed away first.

Country music is notorious for its sentimentalism. There was a song we used to sing about a dog called Old Shep. I think it would apply to Mickey.

If dogs have a heaven
There is one thing I know.
Old Shep (Mickey) has a wonderful home.

12.
The Wind Pump

A red two-story granary stood next to the wind pump before it, too, burned on that fateful day of October 15, 1938, when the barn burned. After that the wind pump stood alone, on the very crest of the hill, halfway between the hog stable and the new barn. A water tank was set next to the wind pump from which the cows drank coming and going to the pasture during the summer.

We dipped buckets into the tank to water the hogs. To the south of the entrance into the hog stable stood a wooden barrel, the slop barrel. With water we mixed ground grain with all the leftover garbage from the house into what was called and deserved to be called slop. It was bucketed into the wooden V-shaped hog troughs. This was called slopping the hogs.

The Ranly farm never had a silo. The wind pump was our landmark, our Eiffel Tower. Our wind pump was not a particularly high construction because it stood on the very summit of the barnyard hill. It caught the wind from every direction, especially the dominant wind from the west and the southwest. Climbing the wind pump was strictly forbidden to us kids and, therefore, was a constant, thrilling temptation. On the very top was a wooden platform. Standing on the platform, the older brothers would oil all the working parts of the big wheel. I do not remember Dad ever climbing the wind pump.

A working wind pump is a mechanical wonder. It is one of humankind's most enduring inventions. The ecologists see it as a permanent alternative source for energy for the future. In my trip to

Tanzania, East Africa, I was thrilled to see ordinary wind pumps supplying water to local villages and for the people's cattle.

I presume the well for drinking water was drilled into the water table the same time that the blue-gray iron tower was constructed above it. For us, the well and the wind pump were simply always there. What was pumped out was drinking water, but so saturated with chemicals that to call the water hard was like calling water wet.

I do not profess to understand even the simple mechanics of a working wind pump. I remember that a wire dangled from the wheel and was tied up to one of the four major supports. When the wire was jerked, the wheel was released, the wind blew the flat, broad vane away from the current so that the wheel itself faced broadside into the wind. Then the wheel began turning. The turning of the wheel worked the arm which worked the pump which brought up the water which filled up the tank. Then the wire was pulled taut again, shutting down all the working mechanism of the wheel.

Then came the electric motor pump and the pressure water tank. I don't know what came first: the desire for piped water to the water tank in the barn, to the hog stable, to the chicken house or the decision to have an inside toilet in the house. It all appeared in one package. The motor and the pressure tank were placed at the bottom of the shallow well under the wind pump. The new system used the original drilled well, drawing on the same water supply. As far as I know, all is the same to this day.

We were by no means among the first to have indoor plumbing. In those days an item appeared in the Cassella news column of the weekly Mercer County Chronicle whenever a family was installing indoor plumbing. Putting a bathroom inside our log house was not an easy thing. We were told that the runoff water from our small cesspool would be so clean that it would not contaminate the creek. I'm not sure I believe that.

All this new technology meant that the wheel and the pumping mechanism of the wind pump were now obsolete. They were dismantled. But the tower still stood. It became the support for Paul's (and later, Orville's) martin swallow houses. Maybe we had martins while the wind pump still worked. But I remember best the three white painted martin houses sitting on the third tier of the wind pump like miniature apartment houses. Martins became a part of the Ranly family stories.

The arrival of the first martins around the end of April was announced with much more enthusiasm than the spotting of the first red-breasted robin. When dozens of pairs of martins arrived and built their nests we knew summer had arrived. Soon the fledglings would be sticking their heads out of the bird house holes and then sitting, haltingly, on the perches, fearful of flying. The older birds would push the little ones off the perches. It was sink or swim, fly or fall. And the little ones flew.

Towards evening there was a gaggling and a cracking and a cawing and a screaming like the background crowd noise to a radio broadcast of a baseball game. The parent birds could be quite protective of their brood and they would come dive-bombing over our heads like P-38 fighter planes. During the mulberry season the martins' droppings turned purple, a strange sight indeed. By the beginning of August, almost unnoticed, suddenly the martins would disappear.

In the same way, the last tiers of the wind pump disappeared. One thing I miss, I think, is not so much the wind pump but the martins. Oh, there are bird houses standing on poles and hanging gourds may attract a few pairs of martins. But it will never be the same swirling masses of martins we used to see around the wind pump.

What I miss most about the wind pump is not exactly not seeing it stand there, with its weather vane and its big fanned wheel. What I miss is that rhythmical sound of the pumping, the screeching of the wheel, and the pumping, the rhythmical, automatic self-mechanized pumping. I miss the rhythm of its pumping.

13.
Farm Work

Farming for our generation was caring for animals, cultivating the land and harvesting. It was all of that and so much more. Small family farms were necessarily diversified, so that if one crop failed, there were others; if the price of hogs dropped, we had eggs and milk. Cultivation and harvesting had its own machinery, machinery much simpler than now, but each piece required maintenance and repairs.

Then there was also the upkeep not only of the house, but of the many other buildings: roofs, siding, painting, The land needed drainage; proper tiling was a major preoccupation. Today with one-crop capitalist farming and with huge specialization in eggs, or fryers, hogs, milk, beef cattle, the whole infrastructure of farm life has changed.

For example, today there are no fences. This is a new wonder for me. Driving through our part of the country now I see no fences. Our 86-acre farm had some nine fields and every field needed fences secure enough to hold in cows, horses and pigs. With the new barn, around the straw stack and cow yard, there was a wooden fence. (We loved to tight-rope walk the top boards.) Along the north and west side of the creek was the hedge fence which was a reality all its own with its own problems. I remember an Abraham Lincoln type of rail fence along the east side of the woods and the north side of the orchard. But mostly the fences were wire wicker fences, with smaller openings near the ground so that the smaller pigs could not squeeze through.

Stretching a fence along a lengthy fence line, say, almost a quarter of a mile, was quite an engineering feat. First of all, the two end posts must be carefully secured. This was done by planting two very large posts with a brace between them, held together by a strong wire cable. That is, both ends of the fence needed these foundation posts. Then the distance was marked off so that at about every eight paces there would be a fence post.

Posts were either of wood or iron. For a wooden post there was a post-hole digger. It had two large upright handles and two spade-like cutters on the bottom. One pounded the digger into the ground, closed shut the iron spades with the wooden handles and then pulled up the loose ground caught between the cutters. Working it carefully one could make the hole perfectly round. It needed a depth of some two feet or more. Then the post (say, a catalpa tree trunk) was set into the hole and the ground was pounded back into the hole around the post to make it secure.

For iron posts there was a round tube, open on one end, with a heavy piece of iron on the top. The tube was placed over the top of the iron post. One brought the tube crashing down upon the top of the post so that the bottom of the post began to sink into the ground. It took ten or more hard blows to sink the iron post firmly into the ground. One must be careful that the post stood straight and tall. The post-pounder was very smooth on the outside so that the hands tended to slide with the repercussions of the blows. This job produced many blisters.

Now came the large roll of new fence. It was opened on the far end of the field. Every vertical wire was wrapped around the large corner post and tightly tied into a knot with a pair of pliers. Then the wire fence was rolled out along the whole length of the field. At the near end it was attached to an iron rod which had nuts and bolts to fasten every wire of the fence.

There were two chains attached to the end-corner post which hooked into this iron bar on the top and on the bottom. On the chains was an iron handle with a pulling mechanism. One pumped the handle and the chain tightened. First one tightened the bottom chain. Then the top chain. This began to draw the whole fence taut. The process continued. As the fence drew taut, one walked the whole length of the line and pulled the fence up vertical against the posts. The pumping of the handles drew the fence tighter and tighter. That is the reason the two end-corner posts had to be so securely fitted into the ground.

The whole apparatus was left to stand several days. The new fence would begin to sag. Then it was tightened again. Finally, it was judged to be ready. Then one cut all the horizontal wires and brought the loose ends around the end-corner post. One by one these wires were tied into snug knots with a pliers. Then the fence could be secured to all the posts along the line.

With wooden posts, one nailed the fence to the posts with staples (which we called steeples). With steel posts, one wired up the fence with wire clips. At last, one released the chains and removed the iron rod. The new fence was as taut as a violin string. Then, across the top of the fence a barbed wire was strung with the same chain mechanism. The barbed wire discouraged long-necked cows and horses from trying to reach the greener grass on the other side of the fence.

If small pigs squeezed through the bottom of the fence, one had to make small wooden stakes, pound them into the ground at the very spot and nail the bottom wires tightly to the stakes very near to the ground.

Line fences which separated our land from our neighbors were the mutual responsibility of both parties. We had line fences with only three distinct sets of neighbors because our land ran up to township roads to the east and to the west. We understood very well that good fences make good neighbors. Each set of neighbors had their own peculiarities which we learned to respect.

Another item of farm work was the upkeep of lanes and roads. We had a wagon called a gravel bed. It was made up of a frame set upon four wheels into which fit the two sides and the two ends and a number of loose poles that made up the floor of the wagon bed. When assembled it looked like a wagon made up of match sticks, but all the parts were movable.

A team of horses pulled the gravel bed to a bank of clean sand/ gravel along the creek. With shovels we filled up the wagon bed. It was pulled to some major pothole in the lane or to the perpetual mud hole behind the woods where three gates opened into three different fields.

Then the whole bed was taken apart piece by piece: the back end, the front end, the two sides. The sand/gravel fell to the ground. Then all of the bottom floor poles were pulled loose. The sand/gravel kept falling to the ground. The wagon was pulled free. The new gravel was leveled smooth. It was a wonder in simplicity and efficiency, road graders, bulldozers, high lifts, backhoes, well, yes, they work, I guess. But our work had so much more the human, personal touch,

But then, maybe I should not slight the operators of big machinery. In the mines of the Central Andes of Peru I got to know the operators of some of the huge mining machinery. They felt so proud, so personally involved in their work. And with good reason. How could our gravel bed wagon play up against a front loader which in one sweep dumps tons of rock-minerals on a huge dump truck? We did what we had to do with what we had at that time. No one can ask for more.

Farm work for the girls included cleaning house, baking bread, doing wash and cooking—cooking by starting with fresh vegetables, fruits and meats. The women did gardening, helped milk cows, and worked side by side with the men shocking wheat and oats and harvesting corn.

I remember when the kitchen floor was still wooden boards and the weekly Saturday scrubbing was quite a chore. There were no table linens. The kitchen table was covered with a brightly colored oil cloth. Later, a piece of colored linoleum served for years as our table cover.

The sitting room was covered with an old linoleum which was painted in the spring of every year. The colors varied. Mom learned to use sponges, which she dipped into pastel colors to create her own designs. It was not unlike modern art, but the paint wore off in a year and it had to be done all over again.

When inlaid linoleum hit the market with colors all through its thickness, we were amazed. It did not need repainting. But then the same design stayed with us for years.

We did not know what a carpet was. When did Mom and Dad get a thin carpet in their bedroom? Rugs were throw rugs on the floor next to our beds to step on with bare feet on cold mornings.

Farm work had its discipline, but we understood the logic of what we were doing and why. There was no punching a time clock, no routine assembly line, no supervision by others.

We had the saying: No rest for the wicked. I guess we were quite wicked. The Germans say: Work makes life sweet. But how sweet do you want it?

We were content with the feeling that a job well done was its own reward.

14.
Games

Everybody plays "Hide-and-seek" and so did we. But we had a game called "Wolf" which had its own style. Everyone ran off to hide except the one designated "Wolf." He (She) closed his (her) eyes, with his (her) head leaning against the garage door, chanting in a loud sing-song voice:

"One o'clock the wolf's not here.

Two o'clock the wolf's not here.

Three o'clock....

Ten o'clock the wolf's not here.

Eleven o'clock he's coming near.

Twelve o'clock he's coming.

He's here!"

Then the wolf turned around to start its hunt.

The idea was not only to find each one of the players in their hiding place, but also to catch them—tag them—"eat them"—before they could run back to the base, the garage door. If a player touched the garage door before the Wolf "ate him" he (she) was safe. The game repeated itself until the Wolf duly caught up with all the players. This game was especially good at night under the yard light at the garage.

Everyone plays "tag" and so did we. But we played "Dare Base" around the steel posts of the wash line on the lawn by the hog stable lane.

Those touching the wash line posts were safe, immune to being tagged. This was their base. So they "dared" the person being "It" by edging more and more off their base or even by running to another free base. It was like a baseball runner on first, trying to steal second. "Dare base" gave a nice twist to "tag."

We played "Andy Over" in school by throwing a tennis ball over the

C.K. of A. Hall roof. The team with the ball yelled "Andy." The other team yelled "Over." The first team threw the tennis ball which had to bounce off the roof. If the second team did not catch the ball, they simply had to throw it back with the chant "Andy Over." But if one caught the ball, he could run around one end of the building and try to touch or hit with the ball as many of the opposition as possible while all of them ran around the whole building. Every-one hit by the ball was eliminated from the game. The game went on until one team was completely eliminated.

After the granary burned in the barn fire of 1938 we had no free standing building over which we could play "Andy Over." So we played the game around a parked car in the yard. This made a farce of the whole concept of the game because both sides could always see if the other team caught the ball. Because it was a farce we loved it.

Also we sang opera, especially Rita, while washing and drying dishes in the kitchen. That is, we would sing dramatically to our own melodies to words of a would-be script.

"O woe is me! I feel so sad."

"What is it? What happened? Why so sad?"

"My dear loving cat just died."

"O woe! O grief!"

Sometimes, the script would get more personal. In a dramatic, powerful soprano, Rita would scream:

"If you do not hurry up with washing those dishes I am gonna hit you!"

And in a profundo bass:

"You just try it!"

"Don't dare me!"

"I dare you!"

This was street theater with real live issues at stake.

We gave used tires the names of automobiles. We rolled these "cars" from the house to the barn, down the lane to the bridge and back, even to the end of the lane. Each kid had his/her own tire with its own trademark name. One tire was a Ford, another, a Plymouth, a Dodge. Tires were thinner then, and higher. Hoola hoops were not invented yet, so we did our best with tires.

When a tire ran over fresh dropping from a chicken or cow, the car was said to have a flat tire. The removal of the stain from the tire and the washing of the smell from the hand was "fixing a flat tire."

We boys developed a type of baseball game by throwing a rubber ball or tennis ball low against a wall, so that when it rebounded it bounced along the ground. We scooped up the ball and threw it high against the wall as if to throw an infield ground ball to first base. Catching this rebound meant that the batter was out. We had markings for singles, doubles, triples, home runs. We played games of nine innings against each other in serious competition.

We also developed corn cob ball. One can throw a dry half corn cob with a lot of twists, curves and drops, especially in a strong wind. The batter used a flat wooden bat. One missed swing of the bat was an automatic out. A caught pop-up was an out. Distances were set for singles, doubles, triples, home runs. Three outs and we changed pitcher and batter. The pitcher would develop better and better stuff on his throws.

The batter might want to put men on base before hitting for extra bases. A missed swing, one out. A short hit: a runner on first. A second missed swing: two outs. A hit double puts runners on second and third. A careful swing. It's a high fly but the pitcher catches it. Side retired. No runs.

The game goes on until nine innings or until Dad catches us and scolds us for not cleaning the hog stables.

We made wooden guns which shot inner tube rubber rings. With a tin snips (a big scissors used to cut tin) we cut one-half-inch rubber rings off a discarded inner tube. All tires had inner tubes in those days and the inner tubes, like the tires, were higher and thinner. Then using about a foot long piece of wood, we strapped on a trigger mechanism with its release, using only a few small pieces of wood and several of the rubber rings. These same rubber rings served as projectiles—bullets.

The gun could shoot a rubber ring about fifty feet. But even at close range, it was not at all dangerous. So now, playing "cops-and-robbers" or "war" or "cowboys-and-Indians" took on the marks of reality. We had real guns. One did not run up to someone and shout "BANG!" and then argue about who shot first. One died only if he was actually hit by a rubber ring bullet.

We had no piece of cement big enough to mark off for "hopscotch." But the soft sand to the west of the garage driveway served us very well.

Among the family table games, we played checkers, parcheesi, Chinese checkers. Monopoly was the major league of family table games. Magdalen was in an altogether different league and deserves its own account. We never played chess. With playing cards, pinochle was our first game; euchre, second. We never played bridge. In those days, only a few old people played Sheepshead. They kept shouting about the "Fuchs."

We quickly taught any dumb kid how to play "52 pickup." We threw all the 52 cards of the deck on the floor and told the kid to pick them up.

I would talk about "snipe hunting" except for two reasons. I do not remember snipe hunting as a child. I think it became part of the family tradition somewhat later. But, by the very nature of the game, I am not to talk about it. For those who know about snipe hunting, no explanation is necessary. For those who do not know about snipe hunting, no explanation is permitted. Matters of national security must be respected. Snipe hunting is like "52 Pickup." You learn the game the first time you play it.

The family that prays together, stays together. Very good. But also, I think, the family that plays together stays together and, in a real sense, the family that plays together also prays together.

15.
War

Our parish was in Forty Hours Devotions when the radio broke the news about Pearl Harbor. I was eleven years old. In church, vested in black cassock and white surplice, swinging the thurible in front of the Blessed Sacrament, I tried to understand what this was all about.

We had had two uncles in the First World War whose stories we heard. The present war in Europe was beginning to have an impact. We heard about the Blitzkrieg and the bombing of London. We were making hay when we heard that Hitler's armies had entered Paris. We saw a few movies and so knew something about what the Eyes and Ears of the World was telling the people about the war.

But now, everyone was talking about Pearl Harbor, Japan, Hawaii. President Roosevelt's velvety voice was talking about "a day of infamy." People began using the phrase "for the duration," which I found difficult to understand. We were in war.

Paul was the first to be drafted. Mom had all of us get up before dawn to see him off. It was a strange, sad moment. What was this all about?

Art, as a brash high school senior could talk and talk, but Mercer County, Ohio, was far distant from falling bombs and invading armies. We still knew nothing about Death Camps.

Dad listened religiously to Lowell Thomas every evening. In school, Teacher Eifert procured new maps so that we could study what was going on in Europe and in North Africa and where were all those strange names like Bataan, Okinawa, the Solomon Islands. A neighbor boy was on Guadacanal. Lucille's boy friend, Ben Droesch, was in India.

They assigned Paul to the Air Force. He became a mechanic and won his battle ribbons in the South Pacific. Norbert had a few deferments because of age but finally was inducted into the army. His Dixie Division spent years in the occupation of New Guinea. Art got more than he bargained for, serving in the Navy and participating in major actions in the Pacific. Orville was the fourth to enter the Armed Forces, but late in the war, and was not sent overseas.

When after the war the four came home they posed for a professional photograph, each in full uniform. This is a masterful memorial for the Ranly family and the war. What stuff my brothers picked up during their years of service to the country only they can know. Here I talk about what I experienced about the war.

We had four service flags hanging in the south window of the sitting room, but since we lived so far off the road, only our own company could see the ribbons.

We sang: "When the Lights Go On Again All Over the World." We participated in scrap metal drives. We helped Mom count and separate our rationing stamps. We prayed for our boys, attending Perpetual Novenas to the Sorrowful Mother. (As it turned out, "perpetual" meant for the duration.) In school, we made up scrapbooks for the wounded in military hospitals. On June 6, 1944, "D Day", we heard Bob Hope on the radio give up his comedy routine to be in solidarity with our boys in the invasion of Normandy.

I remember the first time Paul came home on a three-day pass. It was early Fall. I came running home from examining the creek for muskrats. There he was, our brother, in smart military dress, with a cap like that of General MacArthur.

Another time Mom and Dad allowed me to skip school (to the public dismay of Teacher Eifert) to take Paul to Cincinnati, to the big train terminal. There we saw all those lines of people, waiting to depart by individual gates, so many service men and families, like ourselves. I saw Paul kiss Erma, his girl friend. We drove home, quiet, and I tried to understand what it was all about.

Mom decreed that every boy in the service would get a letter from home every week. (Paul says that this must have started later, because he still complains about getting so little mail during his first months of basic training.) The first few weeks went quite well. Even a few months. But the war dragged on. Now there were three, now four men in the service. We made copies, using carbon paper. We complained. Mom said that the experience was good for us, that it would make us all into good writers. Well, I don't know about that.

It was good for my younger sister Ella Mae. She so got the hang of writing weekly letters that later she kept up the practice with Don and me in different seminaries. She changed the format into a newsletter called "The Ranly Rubbish." These pieces became invaluable communiques of everyday life. One year we saved all the letters, put them into a scrapbook and gave it to Ella Mae on her birthday. When her first baby, Terry, was born, in her weekly letter Ella Mae broke out into a pean of joy. We framed the letter and gave it back to her. I think the Liette family still guards these family legacies.

The war came into our home one summer afternoon. I was not there. My sisters tell the story.

Art was home on leave from the Navy. He was serving on an LCI, Landing Craft for Infantry, and had been in several major landings in the South Pacific. On furlough, Art was having his late nights out with his buddies. Now he sat sprawled out on that purple-colored sofa in the sitting room, dozing.

The radio was playing. No one noticed when the program changed from music to a war story. On the radio there was a roar of airplanes and a crash of bombs. Art jumped up with a wild start and began running to man battle stations. The rest of the family was terrified.

The war had come home.

16.
Apple Butter

In a good year, the yellow transparents would be ripe around the Fourth of July. These were soft, sweet, eating apples. Good early apples were harbingers of a good harvest. We searched for the best round yellow apples lying under the trees and carefully ate around the worm holes. The Kempers also had a tree of yellow transparents which leaned over their fence onto the road. We declared that all fallen fruit along the road was on neutral ground and was fair game for common consumption.

Mom would cut the yellow transparent apples into quarters and boil them with their skins in sugar water and cinnamon sticks. We ate them with milk or even put them into milk soup, which was simply milk and bread. We never made apple butter with yellow transparents.

By middle August a number of other apple trees would come to maturity. This inaugurated the apple butter season. No less than three to four bushels of solid round apples were needed.

We had a mechanical apple peeler which was attached to the side of a table top with a clamp and a screw. One stuck an apple through its core on to a three-pronged fork. Then by turning a fly wheel, the apple would turn itself towards a knife-blade and somehow by this thingamajig about ninety percent of the apple would be peeled. The peeling, all curled up, fell into a slop bucket sitting on the floor. Then someone removed the apple, cut it into slices and removed the last bits of peeling.

Peeling apples was a family affair. There would be some five of us or more, each with an assigned task. It took most of a day to prepare three/four bushel baskets of pared, sliced apples. These were covered and kept in a cool place over night, sometimes in the cellar.

Meanwhile, the apple butter kettle had been cleaned. On the outside the copper kettle was black as an iron frying pan, but inside it glowed with a soft orange color, especially when rubbed and wiped clean with a soft cloth moistened with vinegar.

The fire was always prepared on the potato patch, just off the front lawn. The kettle was suspended by its own large rounded handle over a wooden plank. A steady hot fire was tended to under the kettle, using very dry wood so that there was little smoke but constant heat.

The year's first use of the apple butter stirrer required a special touch: to examine it, clean it, repair it. The apple butter stirrer was a relic, reverenced with the same respect we had for cradle scythes, spinning wheels and butter churns. It had a long wooden handle like that of a pitch fork and a flat wooden blade, like a horse's head, full of two-inch holes. When the blade was set into the kettle, it was deep enough to glide along the bottom. One worked the stirrer slowly, with a circular motion, so that none of the contents would cling to the sides of the kettle.

A wooden kitchen chair was set by the fire. The cut apples were dumped into the copper kettle, along with water, sugar and cinnamon sticks. Beneath a wide brimmed straw hat, someone sat stroking and stirring and moving the stirrer for hours on end. The water came to a slow boil. The stirring went on and on, back and forth, around and around.

The individual slices of apple slowly lost their form. The mass took on a red-brown color. It got thicker and thicker, like ice cream coming to term. The experts gathered around to watch, to taste, to test the consistency of the final product. When the apple butter was declared done, the kettle was taken off the fire and set directly on the ground.

Meanwhile, a parallel project was in process. We searched the cellar and came up with five/six brown-red ceramic clay crocks. These were washed in sudsy hot water, toweled dry and set aside.

Now the still hot apple butter was ladled into the waiting clay crocks. These were brought inside to cool and set for a few days. Then Mom melted paraffin, poured it over the top of the crock to seal in the apple butter. Then the top of the crock was covered with a newspaper and tied with a cord string. The crocks were eventually stored in the cellar. Through the long winter, one by one, the paraffin seals were broken and the apple butter served at table and spread on homemade bread to make sandwiches for our school lunches.

To tell the truth, as a family, we preferred pear butter to apple butter and made two batches of pear butter to every batch of apple butter. The whole operation was the same. We used the late summer pears. School lunch sandwiches tasted better with pear butter.

Making apple and pear butter were red letter days during that time of late summer when almost every day was a canning day. In late May or early June a few precious pint jars of wild strawberry jam had been stacked away in the special cupboard in the cellar. Maybe Uncle Sebastian's cherries had been canned, almost as beautiful as strawberries. Some peas, then green beans, mustard beans, red beets, sweet corn, apple sauce. Ball Mason jars were made at Muncie, Indiana, and when the Ranly family stopped canning, the whole company went out of business.

Very special canning days were when the Georgia peaches went on sale in Celina. Several wicker baskets-full of peaches were bought. (The baskets then served to carry wash, that is laundry, and so we called them wash baskets.) Now after wild strawberries and ice cream, the next best things were peaches and ice cream. As I have said, when we dreamed of what heaven must be like, peaches and ice cream were always at the top of the list.

Mom was realistic enough to accept the fact that not all those rosy soft peaches would find their way into a sparkling clean jar. The best of the peaches were consumed on the spot by that assembly-line of workers. Bought peaches in tin cans are really quite good. But they are nothing compared to home-canned peaches. Especially in its setting.

We are in the throes of late January. It is cold, with dark, gloomy days, and school five days a week and on Saturdays we have to haul manure out of the horse stables, and well, life is a drudge. But for Saturday dinner—and dinner is eaten at noon time—there are mashed potatoes, sauerkraut and pork ribs and, for dessert, Mom gives permission to open a can of peaches.

Summer in January.Heaven on earth.

17.
Bees

Dad kept bees. There was a lean-to on the north side of the house, alongside the orchard, which we called the bee stable. In the best of years, it held a dozen or more bee hives. Bees came to play a significant part in our lives.

A bee sting was a major event. The pain, the swelling, the annoyance of it was almost worth the extra, special attention one received. A good bee sting could also serve as an excuse to get out of work.

We came to understand bees, their moods, their rhythms. On bright clear days of early summer, bees were so active, so busy, that we could hoe potatoes right up to the bee stable with no fear. But on hot, sultry days, the bees would get into an angry mood and then watch out!

There were many theories about why a bee stings. One was that when a person is scared, he (she) sweats and bees sting at the provocative smell of perspiration. Those people who handle bees with thousands of bees crawling all over their faces and heads and arms have no fear of bees and therefore the bees do not sting.

So the point is that when a bee is buzzing around your head, buzzing and buzzing and always getting closer and closer, you are NOT to get scared. Now don't get scared, I tell you, or else you will sweat and the bee will sting you. Make yourself like a statue. Eventually, the bee will tire buzzing around you and it will leave you alone. Whatever you do, don't run. Running infuriates a bee. Oh, no! Don't swing at it. Even if you swat it, the bee will sting as it is squeezed below your open hand.

OW! MOM! MOM! A bee stung me! Well, at least now I don't have to hoe potatoes.

The pain of a bee sting is a primordial experience, like the first cry of a newborn baby. There is nothing to compare it with, that first zinging, stinging, paralyzing pain. There appears a suggestion of blood. A little red welt immediately forms a circle around that pin-point where the stinger penetrated the skin. In an hour or so the swelling begins. Wet mud, cold compresses, some Watkins medicine seem to help, but they are mostly weak palliatives because, in the end, one must wait to wear down the pain.

A sting in the forehead will begin a swelling that will close shut at least one eye. To wake up of a morning and look upon the world with only one eye leaves one somewhat bewildered. One could count on Mom's sympathetic touches, but the rest of the kids would tease you no end. Mom would say: "You will get over it." And so we did.

To be stung by a flying buzzing bee has something heroic about it. But to step barefoot on a bee sucking a clover blossom on the front lawn is a sneaky, nasty bit of bad luck. No one said life was fair.

Mom was valiant, brave in the face of possible bee stings, but also quite imprudent. Her biological organism suffered severely from the poison of a bee sting. She became sick for several days, with fever. Strangely, I inherited a number of physical traits directly from Mom, such as two crooked little fingers. I have Mom's biological weakness reaction to bee stings. So excuse me, please, but I will take no chances. You kids hoe potatoes in front of the bee stable while I pick green beans in the garden in front of the house.

Or a different scenario.

Gee, Mom, we would like to hoe potatoes, but the bees are really raging mad this morning. Look how they are flying all about the hives. We better wait until another time.

What we would not tell Mom was that someone had thrown chunks of ground against the bee hives, riling up the bees until they came storming out after us, like Indians on a warpath. This was playing dirty pool and maybe I should not tell tales against ourselves. But we are all children of Adam and Eve and the Ranly clan certainly was not an assembly of saints.

Then there were the days when the bees swarmed. We would hear all the commotion. At a safe distance we watched all the movement around a particular hive. The swarm, a black snarling cloud of buzzing bees, would begin to move across the garden. Dad would have us watch it, to see where the swarm would land, perhaps on a tree limb or in a hollow fence post.

Dad would set an empty hive below the spot where the noisy mass of live bees, about the size of a large football, had landed. Then Dad rolled down his long sleeves, buttoned up his shirt and put a bee net over his straw hat. He would shake the swarm to the ground in the hope that the queen bee would find its way into the clean empty hive. The bees, of course, would follow the queen. The hive would stay at that place for some time. And then, in the dark of night, Dad would bring the hive back to the the bee stable and life would return to normal with one more functioning hive of bees.

To take the honey from the hives Dad again dressed up in the bee netting. But now he had with him that most magical of instruments, the bee smoker. This was a small wooden air pump, like a foot pedal to a house organ. Small rags were soaked in kerosene (which we called coal oil) and set on fire, creating a blue, acrid smoke. The smoker had a small tin hole at the front end, like an exhaust pipe. The smoldering rags were put into the back. The bellows of the pump were worked by hand. Smoke came bellowing out the front like an exhaust to a motorcycle.

Dressed like a zombie and armed with the bee smoker, Dad approached a set of bee hives. Over the summer two or three boxes, one set on top of one another, were full of fresh honey. For the fall and winter the bees could survive with only one remaining box. The smoke momentarily paralyzed the bees, but they suffered no permanent harm. Dad worked slowly and calmly at his task.

As the boxes were brought into the house we set to work. A bee box is divided like a file cabinet, with wooden frames, set side by side. The frames were pulled out, one by one. As I say, it was like pulling files from a cabinet. And there we had another of nature's miracles.

Next to a snowflake is the beauty, the perfection, of a honeycomb.

Criss-crossed lines of perfect hexagons, dripping with soft, brown sweet-smelling honey. Licking Mom's mixing bowls could not be compared to sucking a finger dipped into fresh honey. A thin knife, heated in hot water, cut the wax honeycomb cleanly away from the wooden frame.

We were not all that professional nor careful in the honey business. All was for family consumption. It never bothered us that bits of bees wax would cling to our teeth while eating bread spread with honey.

I must tell you about how bees got drunk. There were those few hot days in September when summer returned with a fury and school was pure torture. We walked home in the afternoon heat, dragging our lunch pails and quite content to lounge around doing nothing. We watched the drunk bees.

By the garage in front of the chicken house were four big trees of summer pears. Their season had already passed. Now lying on the ground were overripe, rotting pears, yellow brown pears, oozing a sugary juice, which by nature's own process had fermented into a sticky alcoholic mass. Honey bees smelled only the sweetness of the overripe pears and seemed innocent of what the consequences would be in sipping the fermented juices. They simply became drunk. Their flying was impaired. Toddling, dizzy, they walked wobbling and unsteady. Stinging was the last thing they wanted to do.

It is a case of nature's exuberance, nature's own bacchanalia. It was Noah intoxicated, unconscious in front of his family after the flood. It was Dionysius in his cups. We studied them carefully, these busy, industrious creatures, these annoying stinging bees, now humiliated and brought low by nature's own rules. Drunk bees made a last instructive footnote to the passing of summer.

Sophia M. Speck
Peter N. Ranly
Married May 1, 1912

Offspring (in order of birth):

Alvina..February 22, 1913
Norbert..March 4, 1914
Victor..December 23, 1915
Hilda..June 2, 1917
Loretta..December 16, 1918
Paul..April 14, 1920
Walter..................................July 28, 1921 (died at 2 yrs, 9 mos)
Lucille..August 6, 1923
Arthur..December 24, 1924
Orville..April 2, 1926
Rita..June 3, 1928
Ernest..February 19, 1930
Mary Ellen..........................March 25, 1931 (died when 12 days old)
Joseph..............................May 13, 1932 (died when 18 days old)
Ella Mae..May 30, 1933
Donald..November 4, 1935

18.
Dahlinghauses

Our town of Cassella, Ohio, had its Church and priest house, its school and teacher's house, a social hall, a blacksmith shop.

Our town had its general store and saloon. These two were in the same building and its proprietors were Joe and Mary Dahlinghaus.

The actual history of Joe and Mary Dahlinghaus would make up a good soap opera. I do not have any documentary evidence about them. What I know is what was common knowledge throughout our part of the county.

Joe Dahlinghaus was a local Mercer County young man advancing towards permanent bachelorhood. Through mail correspondence he found a parallel case of a lady approaching an unmarriageable age. The lady found her way to Ohio, the two were married, had no children and ran the Cassella store and saloon for several generations.

The building had two stories, covered with a light gray artificial shingle, and had a porch running along its front, facing Highway 119. The east side of the saloon had no window and stood right up against the sidewalk.

For years there was a high standing red gasoline pump along the highway side of the store. To serve gasoline to a customer, Joe Dahlinghaus would step out of the saloon, insert the hose into the car's tank, pump gasoline by hand, moving a long handle back and forth. We watched the gasoline bubble and run through a glass bowl at the top of the pump and from there, somehow, flow through the hose to the car tank.

From the porch-highway side, one door opened into the saloon, where Joe alone was in charge. The saloon had a second door, on the east side, facing the church.

On Sundays, the women and children went to church early and prayed the Rosary. The men went to the saloon, presumably to talk about neighborly things (butchering, threshing and the like) but mostly to smoke and maybe have a drink. When Teacher Eifert rang the church bells, the men would walk, single file, out of the saloon, up the sidewalks and into church. After Sunday Mass, the kids found a Sunday paper and began reading the funnies in the car. The women stood in front of church, talking. All the men returned to the saloon. There never was a pastor strong enough to break this custom.

The second door from the porch-highway side opened into the store. Here Mary Dahlinghaus ruled. A large passageway between the store and the saloon contained a low freezer with treasures we all prized: ice cream. To the left of the store were high shelves, touching the ceiling, loaded with merchandise of all sorts. To the right was the candy show case and beyond that a wooden counter. The living quarters were to the south, beyond the counter; the bedrooms were on the second floor.

The customer was always met by a clerk who personally brought to the counter every item on the shopping list. No self-service here. There was a large storeroom to the west. As the customer read off an item from a list, the clerk would disappear and come back with the precise order: trademark, size, number, whatever had been requested.

There was an ice box with cheese and cold meats on display. A hand-turned meat cutter sliced off thin, round pieces of bologna. Mrs. Dahlinghaus was always on hand, supervising all the proceedings. She had the good will to offer us kids a choice of candy from the glass case near the door.

Joe and Mary Dahlinghaus made an unusual couple. Joe was anything but the friendly, smiling, garrulous bartender of the traditional neighborhood tavern. He was taciturn and severe. Youth would mark on the wall calendar behind the pot-bellied stove the days when Joe

Dahlinghaus smiled. Yet he was honest and trustworthy at all levels and ran a good business. After all, his saloon was the only show in town.

Mary Dahlinghaus put on the demeanor of a rather refined lady, which, indeed, she was. Coming from the German city of Cologne she could talk about the beauty of its majestic gothic cathedral. She spoke a literate high German, in contrast to the Platt Deutsch of most of our neighbors and the dialect of the Ranly family. (Our family came from about 150 miles up the Rhine River from Cologne.) Mrs. Dahlinghaus suffered very much over what happened to her Fatherland during the Second World War. She never returned to her homeland.

Mrs. Dahlinghaus was a very devout Catholic, attended Mass daily, and, if I dare to interpret what was going on between her and the parish priest, I think she was somewhat scrupulous. She tended to supervise the moral level of the whole community, family by family.

So where does the Ranly family fit in all this neighborhood gossip? For one thing, on Sunday afternoons, Dad tended bar at the Dahlinghaus saloon. He put on a white striped shirt with a thin tie, rolled up the long sleeves with a rubber garter and was quite the dashing bartender.

Of a summer Sunday, when the Cassella Owls baseball team played at home, the saloon was a busy place. I know. During the baseball games I chased foul balls or kept score on the left field scoreboard. The treasurer of the Owls, Arnold Cron, would walk up and down the wooden bleachers with a cardboard cigar box, asking the adults the price of admission. I think it was a quarter. At the end of the game he paid us boys a dime apiece for our work. With this dime I walked into the saloon, bought a cup of ice cream and a bottle of Pepsi.

Pepsi Cola hits the spot.
Twelve full ounces that's a lot.
All of this for a nickel, too.
Pepsi Cola is the drink for you.

And several Ranly girls worked in the Dahlinghaus store, especially Hilda and Lucille. First Hilda. She was like a live-in maid and turned over to Mom and Dad the three dollars a week she earned. I do not remember when this started. I took for granted that one or both of my sisters would be serving as clerks behind the wooden counter. We got no special favors from them. But Mary Dahlinghaus was generous to a fault. At least, generous with candy to treat children.

And then I had the job for several winters of carrying firewood for the Dahlinghauses. The cut firewood was stacked in the barn/garage west of the store, near the right foul line of the baseball diamond. The heating stove in the living room in the back used mostly cracked coal. But Joe Dahlinghaus preferred firewood in the pot-bellied stove in the saloon. So every day I had to fill the wood box along the wall.

It took eight to ten trips, from the barn, through the length of the front porch, then into the saloon. Carrying firewood has its tricks. It is a balancing challenge of sorts. You had to carry only so many pieces of firewood so that you could clasp your two hands together over the back. The wood had to be carefully stacked so that the maximum number of pieces would fit in the box behind the stove.

One day the seminarians were on a free day and were eating and drinking in the saloon. Mary Dahlinghaus, as was her custom, was treating them royally. When I came in with an armful of wood they tossed the wood any which way in the box. I was delighted. I made three less trips that day to the woodshed. Joe Dahlinghaus did not have the nerve to interfere.

My daily pay was a nickel; sometimes, an extra tip. I saved the money meticulously. Yet, sometimes I splurged in buying a nickel candy bar, such as a Milky Way. The ultimate candy bar was a ten cent Mounds bar. It came in two pieces, coconut white in the insides, covered with chocolate and with an almond nut on the top. If heaven cannot be peaches and ice cream, let it be a Mounds candy bar.

In time, a local couple bought the Dahlinghaus store and saloon and kept it running until supermarkets and home television changed the lifestyles of the local community.

Then the place fell on very hard times, very sad days. It became a seedy, rowdy tavern. I am glad I did not live near to see the time of its disgrace.

Finally it was abandoned.

Only in the spring of 2000 did the highway department have the building razed. I look at the spot of ground. It is so small, say, in comparison to ranch houses and the new houses of today. How could so many things have taken place on such a small piece of ground? It is hardly the size of a respectable onion patch.

19.
Pickles

It came as a great surprise to me that the botanical names for the plant and for its fruit is CUCUMBER and that TO PICKLE is to cure meat, fish or fruit in some salty brine or vinegar. To us, the plant and its fruit were pickles and a really big pickle was a cucumber. To prepare or to cure these green, oblong fingers, Mom would say: "We have to MAKE pickles," "Today we will make sweet pickles;" "Let's make bread-and-butter pickles."

The pickle patch was something extra, thrown in between the family garden, two big lots of potatoes (early potatoes and late potatoes), the cane patch and perhaps a small lot for melons. Pumpkin seeds were mixed in with the corn seed and the pumpkin plants had to survive on their own, hidden under the shadows of the growing corn plants. What a surprise when cutting corn to come upon large ripening pumpkins! All vegetables, fruits, cane molasses were for family consumption.

Pickles were our only money crop. The money was primarily for us kids, especially to buy school supplies at the end of August. Pickle money was to us little kids what muskrat trapping money was to the older boys: spending money in our pockets.

Pickles had become an established tradition. We had a number of regular clients who came from as far away as Minster. Some years we put ads in The Mercer County Chronicle. When buyers came, we stood around, bashful but curious, and gawked at their style of car, how the people were dressed, how they talked as they examined our selection of pickles. Some buyers wanted only little ones; others bought only the big ones—"cucumbers."

Once a pickle plant, with its several vines, begins to spread out over the ground, cultivation is difficult. Mostly, you must pull out the weeds as they begin to stand out above the plant's leaves. Bees visit the yellow star-shaped flowers with great diligence. By the end of July, the small pickles begin to appear. And then, every two days, a major job is picking pickles.

You must step gingerly so as not to crush the tender vines. You must look carefully up and down every vine. Pickles seem to have a knack of hiding themselves, like some fleeting lizard, doing a kind of disappearance trick among the vines.

The best-sized pickles are the size of a large forefinger, but, as we saw, some buyers prefer the very small ones. The big ones we found were proof that the people who picked this row of pickles the last time missed some good ones and now they are overgrown.

Picking pickles was where we learned to count in German. Eins, zwei, drei, vier, fünf....We could move up and through the thousands in German.

We had some strange concepts about numbers. After all my studies in philosophy I am still mystified about how we kids thought about numbers. For example, when an argument ended in bets (which was often):

"I betcha!"

"How much?"

"I bet you a thousand dollars."

"Well, I bet you a hundred thousand dollars."

"I bet you a hundred million dollars."

"I bet you the highest number in the world dollars."

"I bet you the highest number in the world TIMES the highest number in the world, TIMES the highest number in the world...."

What is this? Infinity? Not exactly, because there seems to be a definite highest number in the world, an actual defined number. But you multiply that by itself! Is this infinity TIMES infinity? I wonder if Saint Augustine could match us with his musings over numbers.

Standing: Sister Teresa Joseph (Loretta), Norbert, Alvina, Father Victor, Ernest, Paul, Hilda, Arthur, Lucille, Orville.
Sitting: Dad (Peter Ranly), Donald, Ella Mae, Rita, Mom (Sophia Speck).

The washline.

Nativity of Mary Church, Cassella, Ohio, as seen from the front yard
at the Ranly home.

The Ranly log house in its second renovation.

Garage and smoke house. Ranly house in the third renovation.

The homestead as it looks today. The fourth renovation

Homeplace renovations.

John Schmidt and Dad, with horses Sam and Sal.

Here we have the John Deere tractor and not horses but, the old
hay loader. Dad, Don, and Rita.

Dad playing with Mickey.

The big red barn, granary, and the wind pump.

Norbert, Paul, Orville, and Arthur.

Lucille and Mom planting in the garden.

The new red and white barn with the machine shed newly painted. All the cows have names such as Zebra, Reddy....The straw stack is an example of a very poor stack, which we called a "pancake." The top of the wind pump looks over the top of the barn.

Don milking the cow.

Our great garden and Mom's flowers growing all the way through and between the triple row of strawberries, the garden and the potato patch.

On Grand Lake by Brandon's Landing. Art and Rita standing; Ernie,
Vic, Ella Mae, Lucille, Don, and Loretta (Sister Teresa) sitting.

Peter and Sophia Ranly's 25th wedding anniversary. Alvina, Norb,
Mom, Loretta (Sister Teresa), Dad and Fr. Vic, Art, Lucille, Ella Mae,
Hilda, Orville, Paul, Rita, Don and Ernie

We always had our family tomato patch, but in contrast to many neighbors, we seldom had enough tomatoes to sell. Pickles were our cash crop.

Picking tomatoes created a new environment, a deliciously tempting one. First of all, there were those green, squishy, horrible tomato worms. Being barefoot, how would a kid kill a tomato worm? Secondly, over-ripe rotting tomatoes were made by nature to be thrown. By whom and against whom? We were the innocent victims of circumstances. So someone got hit by a rotten tomato! I have no idea who threw it. Who? Me?

We also threw clods of ground which we called chunks. Many times a chunk fight moved on into the high standing corn. This was real sport, with all the excitement of a battle field.

A chunk of ground falling on standing corn sounds like a hand grenade with flying shrapnel. You hear one land to your left. You know the thrower is near. You launch your own missile and run. A new barrage falls, coming from a different direction. A chunk fight in high standing corn is more fun than hockey/soccer/football put together

I do not remember eating raw pickles in salads. They were all "pickled" into bread-and-butter pickles, sweet pickles and the like. Some were canned; others preserved in brown gallon crocks in the cellar. Only in advertisements did we read about dill pickles. When I tried my first dill pickle I did not like it. Mom also prepared a green pickle relish which we ate on hot dogs and hamburgers. The sweet pickle relish you buy in small jars tastes remarkably like the relish Mom made.

Then there was sauerkraut. Cabbage also came to head in late July. We watched every plant with great care so that the cabbage head would not crack open with size or age. With a large butcher knife we cut the head off from its bottom leaves and its roots.

When there were on hand a dozen or more cabbage heads, about the size of footballs, Mom got out the big wooden grader. And again the wooden wash tub was put into service. The grader was set at an angle into the tub, and half-heads of cabbage were pushed up against the face of the steel blades. The cut cabbage fell into the tub. The hard center core was tossed aside, but actually the core was quite sweet and tasted good.

Of course, we ate cole slaw which is cut raw cabbage in a sweet/salt milk dressing. But the major part of garden cabbage was to become sauerkraut. The big white ceramic crocks that were kept guarded in the southeast corner of the cellar were carefully cleaned.

Mom firmly packed the cut cabbage into the very bottom of the ten gallon crock. Then she sprinkled on a white coating of coarse salt. Then another three/four inches of cabbage. More salt. Near the top, she placed a smooth rounded piece of wood which was made to fit loosely into the crock. On top of the wood, a heavy rock. The salt drew out the juices of the cabbage and there began a fermentation process which in some two months resulted in sauerkraut. I guess you can call sauerkraut pickled cabbage.

Sauerkraut made our Saturday dinners. Ordinary folk like us ate dinner at noon, maybe an afternoon lunch; we had supper at night. That is how God ordered the universe. Any changing of these names or hours is against the established order of things.

On Saturdays there was no school, but we had lots of work, both inside and outside. The whole family would be sitting around the kitchen table as the Cassella church rang the noon Angelus. All were seated in their proper places. Quiet everyone! Some one was asked to lead the praying of the Angelus. The littlest of us could mumble through that most unintelligible prayer: "Pour forth, we beseech you, O Lord, your grace into our hearts...."

Then, to the attack. Mashed white creamy potatoes, spare ribs and sauerkraut, with molasses on homemade bread. This is what living was all about.

In 1965, as an ordained Deacon, I was visiting the sick at Coldwater Community Hospital. I came upon an old Cassella parishioner, Mrs. Joseph Boeke, the mother of three priests and two religious Sisters. Totally disoriented by the hospital routine, the poor lady was depressed and in poor spirits. And to top it all off, she complained, "I've been here over a week now and not once have they served me sauerkraut!"

I can feel for her. What has this world come to when the only pickles we get are from Burger King. And, please tell me: where can I get some good, honest, wholesome sauerkraut?

20.
The Cane Press

September, Labor Day, the first day of school and black smoke was coming out of the high chimney at the cane press. The Frank Feltz boys continued their family tradition to press and process the juices from sorghum cane into molasses. This was as close as Cassella came to industrialization and a factory.

From home, we walked past the cane press every time we went to town/church/school. From our yard we could see the chimney and the smoke. As a business, the cane press belonged to the Feltz family (though our brothers Norb and Paul worked there some years). But as a tradition, a legend, a culture, the cane press was woven into our family life.

For, of course, the Ranly family grew cane. I understand that it is a type of sorghum. We knew that it was not sugar cane. We called it molasses cane or just simply cane. Our patch was always next to the big patch of late potatoes, next to the corn. It sprouted green along with the field corn. When the cane was five/six inches high we had our first task: to pull suckers.

From one seed a major trunk would grow straight up. But around its edges several off-shoots would sprout. If left alone, the whole hill would grow into four or five half-grown stalks of cane. The idea was to have that major trunk grow straight and tall into a single stalk, rich and succulent in juices. The small off-shoots are called suckers; they are like parasites. They must be removed when very small.

It was a job made for little kids: pulling suckers. We hated it. The whole task required that we practically crawled on hands and knees the whole length of the cane patch, tending to all the ten/twelve rows of cane. We were always under the supervision of an adult, because the job was rather delicate: not to harm the main trunk but pull off all the suckers. Cane, at even that tender age, has leaves which are very sharp. The leaves can cut your lingers like a razor blade. We often worked with bloody fingers.

The cane grew straight and tall, higher than the corn, unless a wind storm twisted it out of shape. Its tassel was a dark brown/red mass of seeds, formed like a bottle brush. The seeds, I now understand, have their own value, but Dad saved only the best tassels for next year's new seed, which he hung in the granary to dry all winter.

By late August the cane was ready for stripping. This was a nasty job. Stalk by stalk, every last leaf must be torn off, and especially, the brown/yellow part of the leaf where it was attached to the main stalk. These yellow leaves were mostly very low, close to the ground.

So as you can guess, again we little kids had to strip bare the bottoms of the cane stalks, while big people easily ripped off the higher, green leaves. The edges of a half-dried leaf of cane are very sharp. They can cut the hand as swift as a whistle. Again this was a bloody job.

With a corn knife, a machete of sorts, one cut the tassels off the cane and then cut the stalks off very low to the ground. The bare stalks, like bamboo fishing poles, were gathered together and tied into ten-inch bundles with twine string, gathered from the straw stack. The whole harvest of cane was loaded on to the two-wheeled trailer and hauled to the cane press. There it was set out in the yard and the Feltz's stuck a wooden numbered peg into our pile of cane. They would inform us the day when our pile of cane would be processed.

The whole operation of the cane press worked off one fire box. Ordinary lumpy coal, like the coal in the shed next to the school, was shoveled into the open door of the fire box. Those orange/white flames and hissing red coals were as close to Hell as we ever wanted to get.

Steam energy moved the heavy iron rollers which ate up the loose stalks of cane like a threshing machine feeder in slow motion. As the stalks passed through the rollers, juice ran down and through and out of the machinery, and all this juice was piped into some internal tanks where, again, steam was used to set the tanks boiling.

The damp straw/fodder was conveyed on a wide belt to an outside pile, like a miniature straw stack. We had the right to cart home a few loads of cane fodder, which more or less corresponded to the amount of cane we had brought in. Mixed with straw and animal dung, cane fodder made excellent compost.

The Feltz brothers carefully separated the cane juice of each contract so that the amount and the quality of the final product would vary significantly according to the harvest of each particular year. The juice was boiled in flat, shallow pans. Over the hours, it changed colors from white to cream until it turned a deep reddish brown. An attendant skimmed off a yellow foam. The juice began to thicken like syrup, but only the experts knew the moment when to declare that now it was molasses, mature and ready to take home.

Mom had prepared some twenty or more tin gallon cans. We were on hand watching "our" molasses drain out of the boiling pans into our own containers. We gingerly dipped our fingers into the mass and tasted the warm, watery molasses. This was the result of what we saw through planting, weeding, pulling suckers and stripping cane. No wonder it tasted so good.

Mostly, we ate molasses on homemade bread at home. For school lunch buckets, we put pear butter on homemade bread sandwiches; molasses would make the bread very sticky. Then there was corn mush, a type of corn bread, baked fairly solid so that it was not the Southern style of spoon bread. Corn mush was pan fried and covered with molasses and served for breakfast. Mush and molasses go together like a horse and carriage. You can't have one without the other.

Corn bread itself, of course, should be eaten with cane molasses. There is no other civilized way to eat corn bread.

The Cassella Branch of the Catholic Knights of America had their annual shooting match on the grounds of the cane press on a Sunday afternoon before Thanksgiving. We saw the clay birds go flying out of the wooden dugout and explode like firecrackers in the air—sometimes—when the shooter was a good marksman.

There I learned the law of physics: that light travels faster than sound. We watched the activity from a safe distance. We could see the clay bird explode, see the puff of smoke come off the shotgun and only some moments later would we hear the sound of the shot. It was like hearing thunder moments after seeing lightning.

The days after a shooting match we scoured the grounds of the cane press, looking for unbroken clay birds to use as ash trays at home.

These days one must hunt hard to find genuine cane molasses. Some dishes are incomplete without bread and molasses. To this day, in every visit home, by the third day for breakfast, the Flautes will serve me grits or blood pudding and Rita sets a bowl of cane molasses on the table. (The Flautes have their secret source for genuine cane molasses.)

I miss the homemade bread. Molasses on soft baker's bread (even freshly toasted baker's bread) is not the same thing as molasses on homemade bread. But after eating grits with molasses bread I can walk outside, look out over the creek towards the Cassella church steeple, and I can almost see the black smoke coming out of the dilapidated ruins of the cane press.

21.

Father Vic

This is not a biographical sketch of Father Victor Ranly, Priest-Missionary of the Precious Blood, even though he deserves a full book. This is an attempt to describe the impact Father Vic had on all of us as we were growing up.

Psychologists talk about role models or "significant others." Father Vic, in his humble, dignified way, was a giant among us. Walking in his shadow was my sister, Sister Teresa Joseph, also a very significant figure and leaving a lasting impression on us.

I never knew Victor living with us in family as just another older brother. I dimly recall his coming home for summer vacation from college. For me, Victor gave a name, a face, became a real person in that most imposing institution which towered over our lives which we simply called The Seminary.

Local farmers referred to Saint Charles Seminary, Carthagena, Ohio, as: "The priest factory." The impressive neo-English Gothic building of yellow brick lies at the bottom of a tree-lined entrance which bellows out into circular lawns before a high six-cornered dome. For generations it housed more than a hundred young men studying six consecutive years of theological studies for the priesthood.

Equally impressive was the high brick chimney of its power house emitting columns of black smoke. Then there were the long green chicken houses, the silos, the milking barns. On visiting Sundays I well remember the barns where brown Swiss cows stood on cement floors in steel stanchions and we saw milking machines for the first time.

Driving up our long lane, looking to the right of the house and beyond the orchard, we could see The Seminary about two miles distant across the fields. When we were coming east on the road from Philothea, there was a moment when the road seemed to lead directly into The Seminary. Motorists driving past on State Route #127 marvel at the lakes, the grounds, the building of The Seminary. The town of Carthagena (if there is such a thing) is dominated by The Seminary. The pastor of Carthagena church always lived at The Seminary. The Seminary was to our whole area what the Vatican is to Rome. Its importance cannot be overstated.

Now try to imagine what it meant for us to have an older brother living within those hallowed precincts of The Seminary. We felt at home there once a month on visiting Sunday. I remember best the museum on the second floor of the Old Seminary with its birds' nests and stuffed animals.

During Holy Week we attended Tenebrae services in the chapel. The fifteen candles on an elaborate candelabra were snuffed out, one by one, after the chanting of fourteen psalms. Then we sat there in darkness when suddenly, with a loud noise, everyone slammed shut his book of psalms. Then we walked out in silence.

The Lord was praying in the Garden of Olives; the Lord was to be taken prisoner. Oh, how they lived the liturgy at The Seminary. And we were privileged to be so close to all this.

The Seminary was like a spoke in the wheel of all the high-steepled churches of southern Mercer County. On our farm from a good vantage point, say, from the old wind pump, if we could not see forever, we could see at least ten church steeples: Cranberry, Saint Henry, Philothea, Carthagena, The Seminary, Saint Sebastian, Maria Stein Convent, Saint John, Saint Rose and our own Cassella (not counting Chickasaw, because its little wooden church did not have a high spire). In larger concentric circles there was more than double this number of churches in the area.

Over the years we got to know Vic's classmates almost as members of the family. We watched them play baseball; we heard their fishing stories. On Free Days they hiked home with Vic, drank Dad's dandelion wine, sang sing-a-along songs around the piano in the front room. My future priestly life would be singularly blessed by the permanent friendship of many of Father Vic's classmates. Their passing, one by one, leaves me empty and sad in a peculiar way.

Father Vic was a handsome man. Glasses gave him an air of superior knowledge which he justified with quiet authority. He played sports well—basketball, baseball, football, horseshoe. Being left-handed was part of his mystique. Football was quite unknown to us and to see him kick a football from the garage to the barn was a Herculean feat. Later, he became a near champion bowler and a respectable golfer: always the southpaw. Fishing was Father Vic's second vocation.

I think I can safely say that Father Vic thought my philosophy career was a watering down of the priesthood. For him, the priesthood meant pastoral/parochial work. But on a summer fishing adventure in the thick of the Ontarian bush on Horwood Lake, Father Vic was examining with great care some small wild plants. He mused out loud: "I always wanted to study botany."

Here was the master of The Seminary flower gardens coming to own himself. Father Vic was not only a lover of nature; he was a student of nature.

On September 8, 1940, Vic was ordained priest. The night before, around the kitchen table, there was held an informal family council. The agenda: starting tomorrow, how will we address our brother? I was too little to understand all the implications of the question. Some of the brothers had their opinions. But this was not to be a case of opinions. Mom declared that as tomorrow our brother would be: FATHER VIC. And so it came to be. There was little deviance over the years.

The Ordination and First Mass of Father Vic stand out like the Washington Monument on the landscape of our family history. There we were on that magnificent front porch of The Seminary, watching the Cassella caravan of cars passing in front. We joined it with our own car and were led back to Cassella like a Roman Emperor returning from the wars. That is our brother—now Father Vic—blessing the packed church with the towering monstrance.

A classic family photo was taken a week later on the day of Father Vic's First Mass. It is the only formal photo that has all thirteen of us children with Mom and Dad together. Mom and my sister Rita framed and preserved the decorated pillow on which Rita carried the chalice in procession to the altar, flanked by Ella Mae and Don.

A tent had been set up in front of the garage for the afternoon reception. Why do I remember the line of people next to the smoke house, waiting in turn to use the toilet?

On Ordination Day, one car full of family had gone to Saint Claire's Convent, Hartwell, Cincinnati, Ohio, for the first Religious Profession of our sister Loretta as Sister Teresa Joseph. In the Book of Life, Sister T.J. may well have a chapter much bigger than any one of us. But since she had been secreted away to the convent over these years, her person does not appear much in my own little world of the period. Later Sister Teresa and I were to have some good times together.

Father Vic's first pastoral assignments were in Orange, New Jersey, where this midwest farm boy passed himself off very successfully as a cultivated gentleman. He would travel to and from New Jersey by train, often by sleeper, and all this fascinated us no end. This prim young clergyman would step off the train on to the platform in a black suit, black overcoat, black hat, with a white scarf, looking for all the world like the President of the United States.

His stories about New York City, the World's Fair, the subways were like fairy tales to us. For years we had hanging on the wall in our Boys' Room a glossy black-and-white photo of a prize fight between Tony Galenti and Joe Louis. In the photo, Galenti is standing triumphantly over a staggering Joe Louis. It was a photographic miracle to catch that one passing moment in Galenti's career. The photo was signed in favor of Father Ranly by Tony Galenti.

Father Vic introduced us to the wonders of eight millimeter home movies. These remain invaluable documentaries of everyday life at home and of the many family weddings he performed for my brothers and sisters.

Father Vic got on the train with me at Van Wert that day in August, 1944, and accompanied me to Brunnerdale Minor Seminary, Canton, Ohio. We found a seat on the left aisle. The train made its first jerking motion. Father Vic urged me to cross the aisle and wave goodbye to the family.

I went to an open window on the right side and saw standing there a very sad group: Mom, Dad, Rita, Ella Mae and Don. I waved to them. They never saw me. They never waved back. The train pulled away. The family was gone.

I never really got homesick as such. But this sad last view of my family standing there along the railroad track has haunted me all my life. Never have I shared this with anyone.

As a family we were orphaned three times. First, Dad left us all too early. Then we all saw Mom off, praying the rosary around her bed in the Coldwater Hospital. Father Vic slipped away without our knowing about it, certainly without our permission. The absence of each one of them is like a Black Hole, a pure vacuum, that sucks into itself so many memories and which leaves us with so many unanswered questions.

One of the many questions I have is: How's the golf game in Heaven for a left swinger?

22.
Apple Jack

From apples we had apple juice, sweet cider, hard cider, apple jack and vinegar. It is something like a biblical genealogy: one begat this, and this one begat the other one. I am not the one to explain the process which connects all the links in this chain. We did not make or drink apple wine. (Is that the same process as our apple jack?)

We made very little wine. Uncle Sebastian and Aunt Anna had various types of wine (cherry, grape, blackberry) which Aunt Anna served us with the air of being a great hostess. We did make dandelion wine for some years. We kids had to pick buckets full of bright yellow dandelion blossoms. The white milk of their stems left black stains on our hands. There was a formula by which a process of fermentation resulted in a pure transparent drink, pleasant to the taste and with a solid kick of alcohol. Dandelion wine made a good drink.

For cider we used only fall and winter apples. We shook the trees bare and picked up every last apple from the ground. There were not strict criteria for selection. Some had small rotten spots; we knew many of the apples had worms. They were all tossed into buckets, poured into burlap sacks and loaded upon the two-wheeled trailer. The apples were taken to a cider press and the car and trailer returned home with one or two barrels of sweet delightful apple juice.

Freshly pressed apple juice is a sweet, sticky drink, but while appearing to be very innocent, it could produce a good case of diarrhea, which we called the runs. We always were amazed that knubbly, useless, wormy, half-rotten apples could produce such a good tasting drink.

As I understand the process, apple juice left to itself turns into sweet cider, which has a small alcohol content. As time passes, it matures and become more bitter; it becomes hard cider. And finally, it reaches a permanent state of acidity called vinegar.

Sweet cider must be treated with sugar and I do not know what it takes or how long it takes for it to become a permanently good tasting wine which is called apple jack. Apple jack was the favorite adult beverage served by the Ranly family. It was served only to adult company, usually along with freshly popped popcorn, say, during some hotly contested pinochle games in the late fall and during the cold winter months.

All hard liquors were secreted away and used within the family for strict-ly medicinal purposes. Among the men, there was hard drinking at wed-dings, at a few known threshing neighbors' and, I understand, at wakes, but I was not party to any of this. To me, all the stories about bootleg liquor or homemade beer were simply that: stories. None of this is part of my own experience. All the while Dad played the fiddle with Pete Studor's orchestra he maintained his composure, sometimes with difficulty. But Mom knew that if threshing ended at nightfall at certain neighbors', Dad would come home late and sheepishly try to sneak off to bed.

When there was nothing in the house to serve company, the men would drive to Dahlinghaus's with an empty glass gallon jug. They took a few drinks at the bar and came back home with a gallon jug of red/brown beer, with white foam at the top of the jug. It had only a 3.2 % alcohol content ("near beer") and so the beer did not disturb the pinochle games very much.

A trick about serving apple jack is to make sure what barrel to tap. You do not keep close friends if you serve them vinegar.

23.
The Day the Barn Burned

The autumn of 1938 was particularly dry. We were far advanced in our harvesting. On a warm bright Saturday, October 15, we were about to finish shredding the very last of the corn, a better than average crop. The corn shredder was set on the west side of the barn, beyond the wind pump, with its blower filling up the hay mow. They say a spark must have set off a spontaneous combustion. In an instant, the whole south end of the barn was one huge ball of flames. Special effects fire bombs used in today's movies are nothing compared to the reality we experienced that Saturday afternoon.

The day the barn burned changed our lives forever. It was Pearl Harbor, the sinking of the Lusitania, Alamo, the destruction of Pompei, all in one. We knew life with the old barn, then there was that fall/winter of 1938, and then there was life with the new barn. I was eight years old.

I remember the old barn, how the horse stables opened up on the north side. I remember the threshing floor with its gnarled plank floor. I remember wooden flails hanging in the barn, and we experimented with them, trying to imagine how people would beat out wheat and oats grains by beating the straw with these long wooden beaters.

I was on the grain wagon, attending to the bright yellow ears of corn as they fell off the husking mechanism on to the flat grain wagon. The wagon was quite full. Then the awful shout: FIRE! and we saw the reality there all about us. Orville (I believe it was he) drove the wagon full of unshredded corn away from the barn directly into the field behind the machine shed, but the corn on the wagon was already ablaze. He unhitched the horses but most of the corn and the wagon burned in the open field. This prompted some towns people to comment, looking on from their distance, "The Ranlys deserve a barn fire, setting a bonfire like that in the open field." It is so easy to be judgmental from a distance.

There was precious little we could do. I think my wagon load of husked corn simply went up in smoke. When at last the Chickasaw fire department came, it was far, far too late to save the barn and the two-storyed granary to the west. The fire truck ran over and on top of the fence along the lane, first to the south, where it could do nothing, and then to the north, where it was able to get in front of the hog stable and the machine shed to save those two buildings.

The hedge fence caught fire east of the garden and the fire began creeping up to the house. Mom believed all her life that the prayers of the parish priest turned around the direction of the wind and saved the house.

Mom sent the girls upstairs to save some clothes before the house would burn. They lay the clothes on the open ground in the orchard. Later, when they went back to retrieve the clothes, some had black holes from flying sparks.

Rita, Ella Mae and Don were playing with some town kids in Ashman's woods and, thoughtlessly, I went to get them. We came running back but kept our distance and went to the end of the lane where a long line of neighbors' cars was parked along the road. Slowly, we came up the lane, crossed the bridge and found our way to the house.

Victor and a group of seminarians came from the Seminary. After sunset, large groups of neighbors stayed on to watch that the fire would not spread. Dad bought baker's bread and bologna and Mom made sandwiches and coffee and they served the men, carrying around wash baskets full of sandwiches.

I went upstairs and tried to sleep but the dancing flames made terrifying shadows against the north wall of the Boys' Room. I snuck back downstairs, sniffling and scared. The smell of burnt grain haunted us for weeks. In a day or so, neighbors came to drag the twisted, gnarled blackened strips of tin to the field to the west. Slowly the debris was cleared away.

Loretta (later Sister Teresa Joseph) now became the family chronicler. She found herself a common school notebook and kept a daily account of what was going on. It is a feminist history, counting the number of pies and cakes baked every day and noting by name every day who were the neighbor men giving us a helping hand, merely for the price of eating. The notebook remains a family treasure.

Now Dad and the older brothers were looking at barns and planning the new barn. There was never a doubt that a new barn would be built immediately. They came up with a whiz of a design, half the size of the original barn—without a threshing floor—efficient and, best of all, beautiful.

Ben Ruschau and his boys were contracted as carpenters. Construction began immediately. Gravel trucks deposited loads of sand, and the cement foundations were laid. I helped gather medium-sized rocks which were placed within the wooden frames so that they were completely covered by the wet, gray sloppy cement.

Hickory and oak trees were measured and cut down from our own woods as supports or timbers in the new barn. Although Teacher Eifert did not like it, I took off from school on the day of the barn raising. This was better than a three-ring circus. Ben Ruschau supervised the proceedings like a ring master.

For weeks, we had watched the men notch the big beams, drill one-inch holes at precise spots and make little eight-inch pegs, one inch in diameter. Each trimmed timber had its code number. Now began the erection, like putting together a construction from a tinker toy set.

First, the standing beams down the center of the barn. Then those around the periphery. Now the cross beams, each one fitted into pre-cut notches and secured by the wooden pegs. Underneath the juncture of two major beams there were fitted four-by-four supports, like tree limbs from the trunk of a tree, but forming perfect triangles with the cross beams. These, too, were secured by wooden pegs. Every hole, every notch had been well calculated and cut out to make a snug fit. Not a metal nail, not a bolt nor an iron brace was used in the whole construction.

The circus atmosphere was increased by those daredevils walking across the open beams that made up the second floor and the roof, securing the ends, fitting in the same angling four-by-four supports.

By the day's end the full frame of our new barn stood there like a giant praying mantis. How proud and happy were the men eating the big supper served by Mom and the girls. Dad was all smiles. We never knew how much he must have suffered and worried over all the costs of lumber, carpenters, food. The barn was being built!

Putting on the rafters and nailing on the tin roof had to have been a tricky business, but this was all done while we were off to school and I know little about it. The siding was a smooth yellow pine. By Christmas the barn was functioning. But it did not really become our new barn until the following summer when it was painted.

Painting the new barn was a family activity. We all agreed on a red barn with white trim. Paul and the boys carefully measured and marked off all the white trim. The two coats of painting proceeded slowly but with great care. What a beautiful thing it was! So we also painted the machine shed, the hog stable and the chicken coop with the same colors and the same design. But the wood on the other buildings was so old it did not retain the new paint well.

Our new barn, red with a white trim, marked an altogether new era for all of us. The way we made hay, hauled manure, fed the horses and the cows (the cows now had stanchions), all changed. The empty hay mow was an open basketball court, but filled with hay (or straw bails) it changed all our barn games. We could crawl up to the two dormers with their little windows. (We called them dog houses.) One looked out to the west; the other, to the east. Sitting there, looking out over the open country, we felt good about the world.

While Paul was in training for the Air Force at Little Rock, Arkansas, in 1942, from memory, he painted a view of the Ranly farm looking west from the bridge. There sit that red-and-white barn, the other buildings, the house, the catalpa trees in the background. I begged that painting from him and had it with me for years in the Central Andes of Peru. I had some local artisans make a woolen tapestry of that scene and gave it to

Paul. He still has the tapestry in his basement. Finally, I returned the original painting to him.

For me, this scene is a miniature of our life from around 1939 until about 1950. Slowly combines, corn pickers, bailers, milking parlors, and TV would change life down on the farm. It was understandable that in time an addition was made to the barn: the whole first floor was remodeled to include electric milkers, and it was all painted white. And now with capitalistic agriculture all of this stands almost empty and without use.

But the new barn still remains, with overhanging gables on both the south and north ends, a very special distinction in the book of Mercer County Big Barns.

24.
School

Mr. Oscar Eifert was my only teacher for eight grades of primary school. I was the last in the family to have only one teacher. The older children had Teacher Hemmelgarn for all eight grades; four of us, I think, had Teacher Eifert for eight grades. Then school consolidation arrived in Cassella.

In the days of the frontier, the one-room schoolhouse served all the families within walking distance. School buses and consolidation changed all that. The name of Cassella's second school was Harting School (It was always referred to as South School.) some two miles south of Cassella. In 1940 the school was closed; its pupils were bussed to Cassella, where a second room was added to the building, requiring a second teacher.

That year I moved on into the fifth grade. Since Teacher Eifert was elevated to the rank of principal, he taught the four upper grades, so that I completed the next four grades with the same and only teacher.

One can get nostalgic and romantic about "the little red schoolhouse." To tell the truth, the color of our brick building was more orange than red. Then as now, good teachers make good schools. Where there are eight grades with only one teacher a bad teacher could be a disaster. Teacher Eifert, for all his idiosyncrasies, was a good teacher. He was creative and dynamic, maintained discipline and kept the rhythm of the day alive.

All the local schools were public schools, but since everyone in the area was Catholic, there was little separation between church and school. The school day started with daily Mass. We went to the school building, dropped off our lunch buckets and books, and then filed out, two by two, to process into the church for daily Mass.

Father Ivo Weiss had us answering many of the responses in Latin in what was known as the MISA RECITADA. When the choir sang, it gathered around the central pipe organ in the upstairs choir loft. For the Masses on First Fridays, Orville and Rita sang a two-part solo, "Oh Lord I Am Not Worthy." All the boys from the fourth grade on up became Mass servers. After Mass, until 9 a.m. were catechism and Bible history.

Formally then, at 9 a m., the official school day began. The first class was always arithmetic. To this day, I feel that my mind works mathematically only the first hours of the day. I've been programmed that way.

Reading and 'riting and 'rithmatic, but also very good history, geography and civics and the sciences. Teacher Eifert taught us music, how to read and write music, the basic scales. He taught good grammar. I took my high school in a boarding school minor seminary with boys from all over the Midwest. I was amazed to find out that I was so far ahead of many of my classmates in simple grammar, syntax and spelling.

There was a fifteen-minute recess at 10:30. Rushing, we could play a few innings of softball, boys and girls together. From 12 until 1 p.m. was the noon hour. Town kids walked home for dinner. We hurriedly ate the two sandwiches of pear butter bread and an apple or a pear so that we could continue the softball game started during the morning recess. At 2:30 was another fifteen minute recess to finish the game. School let out at 4.

We walked the road and the long lane home, ate a lunch and then worked at chores until dark. Then we ate supper. We had little homework. Teacher Eifert had us do almost all our tasks in school.

When we were eight grades in one room, the average size of a class was five or six, almost fifty pupils all together. Rita was in a class of only three. After consolidation into two classrooms, the average size class was seven or eight.

Teacher knew his students like his own children—and he knew our parents and our older brothers and sisters. If a third grader was a slow learner, in many lessons, Teacher let him limp along with the second graders. If a pupil was a fast learner, he/she could be joining in lessons two or three grades above his/her actual level. I never found school boring.

Then there was the library. Teacher Eifert had an arrangement with the Celina Public Library. Every six weeks he exchanged some fifty books at the various grade levels. That meant that every six weeks we could find entirely new books in the black bookcase in the front of the room. Those of us who could complete our assignments with dispatch had a gold mine of reading material. We could also take these books home. Among the few personal effects saved from my grade school days I have a notebook that summarizes over a hundred books that I read during one school year.

Next to the school building still stands a duplicate building, the C.K. of A. Hall. This had been Cassella's first school. The Catholic Knights of America made it into a community social hall. It had two backboards for two basketball hoops, but the ceiling was so low that basketball and volley ball were very cramped. We school children were not allowed to use the hall very much, not even during the winter or on rainy days.

But we did have the right to use the stage in the C.K.of A. Hall. This was quite a professional stage, well elevated, with pull curtains, footlights, a dressing room and space and material for props and scenery. Our Christmas programs became quite theatrical.

Also, some years during Lent, local youth and adults presented dramatic amateur productions which captured my imagination. One year, the theater piece was a Western drama with the title "The Thundering Herd," in which dramatic action centered upon a passing herd of buffalos. Why do I remember that? Because it must have impressed me very much.

When Cassella school had its own school bus, we Ranlys used it very little. It stopped only at the end of the lane, but walking that far was almost halfway to town and to school. Besides, the timing of the bus route was inconvenient for us. But that yellow and black bus did make the whole school feel very distinguished.

At that time, the state of Ohio required that all youth attend school until sixteen years of age. A few boys in our school had failed a few years and now simply abided their time in the eighth grade until their sixteenth birthday and then went to work on their fathers' farms.

Mom and Dad set the policy for all the older children that they quit school at sixteen and work, either at home or get a job. The only way to escape was to enter the religious life. Loretta got her high school diploma after she entered the convent. I was surprised the first time I heard how strict Dad was at that time. In 1936, Paul had his sixteenth birthday on April 15. He was not permitted to finish out the school year. Dad thought the farm work was that important.

By my time, the boys were allowed to graduate from high school. But what good is schooling for the girls? Lucille got her high school diploma when she was near seventy years old to the great delight of her family and grandchildren. Finally, Art and Orville, and even Rita and Ella Mae, graduated from Saint John's High School, before it became Marion Local. (Or did Ella Mae graduate from Marion Local?)

But it was not for lack of smarts. The few of us in Religious life who had the good fortune of a higher education did quite well for ourselves. But we know that at every level each one of our brothers and sisters is more than a match for us.

They always beat me in Sheepshead.

25.
Corn Harvesting

I will talk about corn harvesting BCP—before the corn picker. I never knew the corn picker as a part of our lives. I was eight in 1938, the year the barn burned, and we already had our own corn shredder. I am surprised that I remember so much about corn harvesting BCS—before the corn shredder.

Even with a corn shredder, the corn must be cut and shocked. This was done early in September when the corn stalks were still a little green, but the kernels on the ears were completely filled out if not entirely hard. The grain would harden and dry in the shock.

First came the bucks. Someone, such as Norbert, would enter a corn field, step off four rows, and, walking between the fifth and sixth rows, count off ten cross-checked rows. At that point, he twisted together the four hills of corn into a cross buck. Around this base, the future cut stalks of corn would be shocked. Then he stepped off another ten rows and tied another buck. At the far end of the field he stepped off eight rows to the left and then, walking down the field, he tied bucks at every ten rows. So when we entered the field for the first time with a machete corn knife, the rows for the future shocks were already anticipated by these rows of bucks.

All the corn was checked planted in rows so that the field could be cultivated down-field and cross-field. Every hill of corn had two/three plants. A good angling blow by a sharp corn knife will slice through all the stalks of corn at one hill in one blow. It's embarrassing to have to make two or more blows.

One embraced a hill of corn with the left arm open, cut with the right, walk up to the next hill, cut it off with one blow and proceed. A big person was expected to gather into his/her arms five hills of corn and carry the armful of stalks to a buck and carefully set them into the growing shock. This is hard work. There are no short cuts, no other way to get the work done.

There was old Clem Albers, stone deaf, but a hard worker. They said that while cutting corn, he carried along a jug of drinking water. He worked so fast, he never lost his rhythm, so that no one could spot the water jug he was carrying.

Actually, we cut very little corn in this way by hand. We had a corn cutting sled which moved on two wooden runners and with a platform the shape of an arrowhead. The two angling sides had two sharp blades imbedded at the top. A single horse pulled the sled between two rows of corn. Two people sat on top of a wooden stool in the center of the sled's platform.

The two people caught the stalks of corn as the advancing sled cut them off from the ground. The horse stopped after every ten cross rows, where the workers carried the cut stalks of corn to the prepared bucks. Then they re-positioned themselves on the sled and the horse walked off another ten rows.

Of course, the two rows of corn in which the bucks had been tied together must be cut by hand. Again, this is hard work. But if the sled could be kept in motion throughout all the hours of daylight a lot of corn could be cut and shocked in one day.

When a row of shocks was completed, someone else came along with a bucket of twine and an open ring tied to a rope. He threw the iron ring around the top of the shock, walked around the shock to find the ring, slipped the rope in the opening and then pulled the rope taut, so that the whole shock began to look like a bundle of wheat. Then he tied a permanent piece of twine string at the height of the rope. He pulled away the rope and the open iron ring so that only the tied twine string held the shock of corn together. And there you have a perfect wigwam of a corn shock.

With the corn cut and shocked there was not as much worry about late autumn rains. But we hoped for drying cold weather after All Saints-All Souls Days to begin husking corn.

You cut the twine string from off the top of the shock. You lay a good part of the shock on the ground. You sit down on your feet and begin pulling the stalks of corn towards yourself, one by one, searching for the big ear of corn, then see if there is a second, smaller ear. You strip away the outer white husks and break the yellow ear off the stalk and toss the ear on the pile that is beginning to form at the base of the original shock. And once in every few hundred ears, you come upon a prize, an ear of bright red kernels.

Most likely you have on your right hand a corn husker. Corn huskers come in various shapes and sizes. The most common is a type of pointed knife, fitted over your fingers like a half-glove. Another style has a big claw that fits over the palm of your hand. The purpose of the corn husker is to tear open the brown-white husks away from the ear of corn and bare it clean so that you can break it off and throw it on the pile of cleanly husked corn ears.

A picture of great beauty begins to take form: rows of brown shocks of corn with piles of bright yellow ears lying at their feet.

Later a grain wagon pulled by a team of horses goes up and down the field. People with tin tubs or bushel baskets pick up the piles of corn and dump the ears on to the wagon. The full wagon is drawn up to the corn crib where a hefty man with a short handled broad scoop shovel tosses all the corn into the corn crib. The stalks of corn, now relieved of their ears, are then re-shocked into bigger, rounder shocks. Then on some later day a hay wagon will come along and haul all the corn shocks into the barn for cow feed and bedding for the stables.

This style of corn husking was all BCS—before the corn shredder. With the corn shredder, the whole operation was parallel to threshing. First the corn must be cut and shocked. Then flat bed wagons brought the cut corn in from the fields and the stalks were fed into the shredder. The cut fodder was blown into the mow; the husked corn fell onto a grain wagon and later was shoveled into a corn crib.

The dream was to have all the corn harvested by the last week of November. After all, with the first Pilgrims and the Indians, that is what Thanksgiving was all about. To give thanks to God for a good harvest.

26.
Autumn

In October, 1999, I visited family in Ohio. It was my first midwest autumn in 26 years. Peru has vaguely two seasons and nothing, nothing that resembles a northern autumn. I carried a camera with me, walking through the woods, driving the car, going fishing. I would stop the car at an ordinary home and point the camera at a bush burning with red and orange leaves. When my family saw the photos, they said: "How beautiful! Where did you take these pictures?"

"In your backyard."

How can we become accustomed to a midwest autumn?

In school we had a green song book that had the song: "I Love September"

"Although summer's over, the bees in the clover

I love September, don't you, don't you!

I love September, don't you!"

With the passing of Labor Day and at the immediate prospect of the beginning of school, we used to sing: "I hate September, don't you!" But childish emotions aside, autumn is the crowning event of the passing seasons.

The first killing frost was dreaded like the Judgment Day. Unless, of course, we were still picking tomatoes every day after school. Secretly, then, some of us were praying for a frost. But the petunias by the house were still bright with colors. The muskmelon vines (cantaloupes to you) were still green and had melons ripening. Dad checked the corn and surmised that the kernels were well filled out so a first frost would not hurt much. Many times, we started cutting corn before the first frost. But the soy beans needed more time to come to maximum grain.

Jack Frost has his own calendar. Yet he sends out his messages. By early afternoon we knew by the nip in the air that this would be the night of the first killing frost. Perhaps there had been a touch or two of earlier light frosts. But a killing frost separates fall from summer like New Year's Eve begins a new year.

Mom dug up and potted the tender, still blooming mums. We gathered in every last muskmelon and watermelon. Well, we'll let the rest of the tomatoes rot. By now we were all wearing shoes. Now we hunted for warm sweaters. The house was warm enough with the gas stove. We would not start the heating stove for some time yet.

By the laws of nature, on this day, the sun sinks golden red in a bright clear sky. The stars are out by the millions (and there were not, in those days, the confusing lights of jet planes streaking through the sky). Dawn is sparkling clear. The green lawns glisten under the white frosting. What was green in the garden begins to turn brown and droop. The leaves in the trees curl up like the closed fists of babies. In a few days the corn will turn a yellow-brown. The soybeans become a golden color. The first killing frost leaves no doubt that autumn is here to stay.

Fall rains can be cold and nasty. But always a few extra days of glorious sunshine shall return—Indian Summer. Sunday afternoon and we are free. Prepare a few brown paper bags full of popcorn. Gather a number of fall eating apples. With the dogs in tow, we take off through the orchard, heading for Ashman's woods.

Along the creek banks there are sumac bushes as red as fire hydrants. On the north side of Ashman's woods is deep green grass, with a heavy cover of leaves from tall standing oak, hickory and maple trees. We roll and tumble through the leaves and come up looking like some Wizard from Oz.

There is a wild grape vine hanging between two oak trees and we play Tarzan with startling realism. The salted popcorn tastes so good with the juicy, somewhat tart apples. We may scare up a cottontail rabbit or two. We look for squirrels. It is a real feat to spot a bushy-tailed fox squirrel gathering nuts for the winter.

We gather bittersweets from the row fence separating Ashman's and our property. Bittersweets are little red berries, about the size of peanuts, which break open with the frost and can be kept indoors in bouquets all winter. We can bear up under another week of school after a good fall Sunday afternoon.

The days get shorter. It may seem that autumn merges into winter without notice. For us, the change was not the solstice on December 21. Nor was it Thanksgiving Day. Winter arrived with All Saints Day.

All Saints Day, November 1, was a Holy Day (not a holiday) but at that time, Catholic communities had no school. There were two morning Masses, just like an ordinary Sunday. Starting at noon on All Saints Day and all through the Second of November, All Souls Day, we could gain the TOTIES QUOTIES indulgences. This means (in Latin) that we could gain the indulgences as often as we fulfilled all the conditions of saying all the prayers in church. This is one tradition I am glad the Second Vatican Council did away with. It's the mathematics, the counting, the external routine that I do not like.

On All Saints Day, like on a normal Sunday, we had Rosary and Benediction in the afternoon. Then on this day we all went in procession to the parish cemetery beyond the baseball field, as if it were a funeral. We processed up to the large central crucifix among the graves where the priest led some congregational prayers. Then the formal procession broke up and family groups looked up the graves of their relatives.

I well remember the year when we were still in prayer by the cross when a big flock of Canada geese flew overhead, honking like a diesel truck, in perfect V formation. Somehow autumn, indulgences, freeing souls from Purgatory are all mixed together in my memories. Do the souls fly to Heaven in a V formation?

November 2 was All Souls Day, but it was also a school day. Some years it could also be the first Tuesday after the first Monday of November: Voting Day. Dad was always on the election board at the C.K. of A. Hall and worked all day on Voting Day.

The thing about All Souls Day was that, along with Christmas, a priest could say three Masses that day. So we rushed though the chores and breakfast to pile into the car to hear as many of those black-vested Masses we could before the 9 a.m. classes began.

If the rest of November was not yet winter, neither was it autumn. It was called the Month of the Poor Souls.

A good name for that time of shortening days and ever colder nights.

27.
Arrowheads

I never found an arrowhead in my life. I envy others, like my nephew Tom Flaute, who have found them by the dozens. Some years ago the Flaute family—my sister Rita—gathered together all the arrowheads, glued them carefully to a piece of wood and framed them behind glass so that now they hang on the wall like a trophy in a museum. There are more than thirty-five arrowheads in that frame.

Arrowheads come in various sizes. Some of them are small and narrow, hardly wider than a paring knife. Others are larger, triangular, some two inches wide on top. Some are almost three inches long. All are made of flint stone, a type of pumice, white, blue, yellowish, almost pink, but mostly a whitish gray. Every stone is sharply honed, a genuine artifact, where the edges had been chipped away by human hands—and only by human hands—until the stone, as we presume, was tied to a straight wooden shaft. And there you have for yourself, indeed, a lethal weapon.

Our farm is only 85 acres. Some of it is in woodland and orchard and therefore has not been cultivated for over 150 years. Most of the arrowheads have been found on our farm in the course of ordinary working of the land. I do not remember finding arrowheads while gardening near the house. Nor have we come upon a cache of arrowheads in one place, as if there had been an Indian village at this spot or some craftsman's workshop.

The arrowheads have been picked up here and there, one by one, over the years, especially by those two/three generations when farmers worked the land personally, ploughing, disking, harrowing, drilling the seeds and then the follow-up cultivating of the corn and the weeding of wheat and oats. Today the work is done with big machinery and, recently, with no-till methods of agriculture and with wheedlers, so that no one comes close to the very soil itself. So no new arrowheads have been found for some time.

How does one understand the number of arrowheads on our own land? All this area had been a forest primeval of hardwoods such as oak, hickory, walnut, ash. How did the indigenous people live within this environment? They were mostly a hunting people, as the arrows testify, on the hunt for smaller animals (squirrels, rabbits, opossums) and birds. There must have been deer, for the deer have returned in the past fifty years. Maybe bear. They were probably a warring people and arrows served as arms against hostile forces.

But how many were they to leave so many arrowheads dispersed over such a small area? How long did they live and travel over this land?

I recall a famous sketch in which a farmer sits by a corn shock, smoking a pipe in front of a backdrop of a setting autumn sun. And as the shadows lengthen and the mists come on, the corn shocks turn into wigwams and Indians dance around an open camp fire.

There are a few mystical days in late fall called Indian Summer with a large yellow harvest moon. This should not be a time of ghost stories or scare tricks. The word Halloween means "Sacred Vespers" or "Holy Night." Originally it was a time for prayers and night vigil before the Feast of all Saints.

In the Communion of the Saints, we tend to be too much ethnocentric, too narrowly Catholic/Christian as if only Catholic saints have preceded us here on earth We should invite and welcome all our sisters and brothers who pass over our land, those who came before us, those with us now and those still to come after us. We should bring Saint John's vision of those multitudes without number before the throne of God in Heaven to our own backyard where we have an open fire, roasting hot dogs.

Perhaps the spirits who dance upon the flickering flames of fire are the very native peoples of these lands.

There should be a way of rubbing an Indian arrowhead, like Aladdin's magic lamp, to have our earth mothers and fathers return to us and join us here, right now, on the one and only Holy Mother Earth we all share in common.

28.
Thanksgiving

I hope it is not blasphemous to say that over the years Thanksgiving became a more memorable family feast than Christmas. Thanksgiving Day meant a rabbit hunt. What I write here is a summary of many memories, telescoped into a few specific stories. Also, these particular stories do not come from my childhood, but from those years when we older members of the family returned home for our annual rendezvous: the Thanksgiving Day rabbit hunt. Norbert would come home from Dayton; Father Vic and Don and I, from wherever we were at the time. Those who lived near home were always on hand.

While philosophy professor at Saint Joseph's College, Rensselaer, Indiana, one year I had to chaperone a college dance the night before Thanksgiving at the old Del Prado Hotel on the south side of Chicago. Faithful Father Ben Meiring accompanied me. After midnight we left Chicago. We drove all night, taking turns driving and sleeping through the snows of northern Indiana. We arrived home just as the family was dressing for morning Mass.

Father Ben left to visit his own family. I went along to church, celebrated Mass, came home to breakfast and changed clothes for the Thanksgiving Day rabbit hunt. One must have priorities in life!

The hunting party would begin to form. Some women would bundle up in hunting clothes. Nephews and nieces served as beagle hounds. The larger kids carried gunny sacks over their shoulders to carry the dead game.

Strategy varied with every hunter. Some years there would still be standing corn. Other years would have been dry with less cover in the fields. Some autumns were wet, with soggy, muddy fields. So would the cottontails be in the woods? In the fence rows? In the open fields? Opinions differed and discussions were loud but unconvincing. At all costs, the army advanced.

The children were spaced between those carrying shot guns. The best shots were on the flanks. Our brother-in-law Ralph Liette was an expert guns man; any rabbit stupid enough to be flushed out near him was a dead goner in seconds. Occasionally we had a real Western circus when an obliging rabbit would run parallel to our front line, say, some twenty yards distant. One by one the shooters would have their shot: a spray of buckshot kicking up dust and snow to the right, then to the left, behind the rabbit, in front of the rabbit. And the rabbit simply ran on and on. I was always cheering for the rabbit.

Then someone would spot a sitting rabbit. This called for a huddle and new strategizing. No one shoots a sitting rabbit? Well, it all depends. Perhaps there is a rifle among us and someone who has never put game in the bag. Well, let him/her have a rifle shot at the sitting rabbit.

But usually, we would line up and designate some teenager, perhaps a girl, to have the first shot. In what direction will the rabbit run? Keep the little kids back! There it goes! The designated shooter waits and waits. It's buck fever! He (she) freezes and never does pull the trigger. The rabbit disappears over the hill. The children/dogs take off running.

Then there was the time that a young lady was designated to have the first shot with a shotgun at a flushed running rabbit. (To avoid embarrassing her I will not use the real name of my younger sister.) But she hesitated and begged to try to shoot the rabbit with the shotgun, even while the rabbit was still sitting. Well, then, go ahead. Boom! Sure shot! Someone approached the kill, pulled it up by its ears and all the rest fell away as pure mush.

December 3, 1954, after I was incorporated into our religious congregation, I was allowed to leave The Seminary and visit family. It was a bright winter day. We were visiting the Flaute family when they still lived in the old priest house of Gruenenwald Convent. Four of us went on a short hunt with one rifle and one shotgun between us. The west woods across the road from the convent house for years was a cow pasture so that it was like an open clean park between the oak and hickory trees.

We came upon a sitting rabbit. We let one of the girls take the first shot with the rifle. Rita was the older. She aimed carefully and pulled the trigger. Nothing happened. The discharged bullet hit the ground so far away that the rabbit never flinched. Ella Mae took the gun, aimed, shot. Nothing. Rita tried again. Nothing. We were laughing like idiots. Ella Mae was taking aim again. Rita was jumping up and down and shouting: "Run! You crazy rabbit! Run!" Ella Mae shot. Nothing. Don went up to the rabbit, kicked it like a football and it took off, running. I took aim with the single-shot shotgun and the poor cottontail rolled over and over upon the winter green grass, dead. Now I never claimed to be a good shot. But I did hit that running rabbit that December afternoon in the west convent woods.

One year Thanksgiving was particularly cold. We decided that, naturally, the rabbits would be seeking the warmth of the heavy brush in the woods. So for hours, our loyal faithful army of hunters beat through any number of brushy wooded areas. We flushed out very few rabbits. Somewhat discouraged, we stopped at the house for a light lunch. But we would not give up.

The cane press field that year was cow pasture. It sported a low green grass. Since the rabbits were not found in the security of the woods, perhaps we will find them in the open fields. The army marched down the lane across the bridge, and we formed ranks in the open field where some fifteen milk cows stood staring at us.

A rabbit jumped up and it was sent rolling. A second rabbit was put away in the gunny sack. Of course, it was easy shooting, like hunting on a golf course. One rabbit had us all shouting as it ran between the cows. But it was also sent rolling. In less than a half hour we bagged eight rabbits from that one clean field. We have the photos to prove it.

By three in the afternoon the winter cold began to penetrate our layers of clothing. We came trudging home tired. Cleaning the rabbits was surprisingly easy and quick with so many skilled hands. The little kids had to hold the rabbits by the hind legs while some adult gutted and washed the carcass. Mom and the women set tables, while carefully tasting and testing all the food, adding the last condiments to the many prepared dishes. (In our childhood days, we did not have turkey, ever, even for Thanksgiving.)

Dinner was a very busy and a very noisy affair with everyone out-shouting the others in tales about some derring-do. Then while the women did the dishes, there were chores to do, cows to milk, hogs to feed.

About 8 p.m. the card games began. Ranlys always play cards with great animation. But on an all-day Thanksgiving Day rabbit hunt, spirits would flag quite early. Family after family would find their winter coats spread out on Mom and Dad's bed. They bundled up their sleeping children, took their farewells and carried out the little ones over their shoulders like sacks of grain.

In the best of days, Dad and Mom would watch all this with a sense of thanksgiving known only to God.

29.
Shoe Repair

Dad repaired shoes. He was not exactly a shoemaker. He sowed up the backs of shoes; he sewed patches on the sides of shoes. Mostly, Dad put new soles on shoes.

I knew three types of shoes: tennis shoes, dress shoes and work shoes, which we called clodhoppers. Tennis shoes—basketball shoes—were made from canvas and cost only a dollar or two. When the canvas tops pulled loose from the rubber soles, no repair was possible. They served only to protect the feet when seining for minnows or craw dads in the creek.

Dress shoes were low-cut Sunday shoes, which were also called oxfords, but the name for us had no association with the English university. Sometimes the backs of the dress shoes tore loose and Dad accused us of not opening the shoe laces as we squirmed and forced our feet into the shoes. Dad seldom put new soles on dress shoes. We simply grew out of them.

Dad resoled our everyday work shoes. He had a whole repair kit which was kept in the attic to the right of the door as you entered the attic through the low-cut door on your hands and knees from the Girls' Room. Dad bought hard, durable shoe leather in two-foot squares. He cut paper models of the size and the contour of the shoe under repair. With a pair of heavy shears he cut out of the shoe leather a piece that corresponded to the size and shape of the shoe.

There was an iron stand whose height came up to the lap of a person sitting on a wooden kitchen chair. Three/four sizes of iron molds could fit over the top of this stand. Dad found the size that fit my sized shoe and slipped the shoe, bottom side up, over the iron mold. Then he carefully cut away the old sole or so carved it down with an ultra sharp curved knife that the new sole would fit snugly upon the shoe.

This took care and skill. Dad treated shoe leather with the same care that we showed a favorite baseball glove. That's a lot of loving, tender care.

Then began the best part. With a mouthful of tacks, Dad began nailing down the new sole with a broad-headed light hammer. The heads of the tacks took the shape of a graceful curved line, like the heads of daisies along the edge of the lawn. The soft brown color of the new sole glistened in the light, outlined with that row of shining tacks. Dad used an iron rasp to smoothen the rough edges of the sole. It became a piece of art. Of course, normally, the soles of both shoes wore out at the same time, so Dad had to make two soles for each pair.

With all the tacks firmly nailed down, Dad removed the shoe from its mold and examined the inside of the shoe. The theory was that the flat iron top would have bent over each tack. If not, there was a type of pliers or pinchers that snapped off the tip of any tack which had not been bent over into the inner sole.

I would take back my pair of shoes gratefully, but cautiously. This was not looking a gift horse in the mouth. Indeed, one must look the shoes very carefully in the mouth. Every nail, its head so prim and trim on the outside, nailed into the bottom of the sole, was a potential land mine.

In time, the tip of any nail could work itself free and lift itself up like the head of a rattle snake. Then it could penetrate through a woolen stocking and pick into the heel of the foot, even if the foot had been so well calloused from the summer months of going barefoot. There is no immediate simple solution to the pain of a nail penetrating the bottom of your foot. Are you going to take off your shoe in school and walk barefoot through the snow?

I'd come home from school and if I couldn't find Dad to make my complaint, I hunted for that shoe repair kit to see if I could pound that pesky little nail down into the shoe leather.

Shoes with new soles were as stiff as a pair of new shoes. But over time they became as comfortable, well, as comfortable as an old shoe. The latest styles were never an issue. Shoes were made to be useful and durable. You either grew out of them or you wore them out to the point that even Dad had to admit any further repair was a waste of time and material.

But May 11 is near. May 11 is Mom's birthday. On Mom's birthday we can go barefoot. So who needs shoes?

30.
The Cellar

Our cellar is below the southern half of the original log house. I don't know when I came to understand the idea of a basement. That a family would play games or almost live in an area beneath the house would mean in our argot that the sitting room was in the cellar. Utterly preposterous! The cellar is where potatoes and sauerkraut were stored, along with the dozens upon dozens of canned fruit, canned vegetables and canned meats.

Walt and Alvina had a cellar outside the house, out by the garden. It had a rounded cement roof, like a bunker, with stairs leading down into the cool darkness below. This was an unusual cellar, but it was, indeed, a proper cellar. Basements were invented much later.

In our day, a major entrance to the cellar was from the front porch. There was a large wooden door that lay flat with the floor. At the far end of the door a rope was tied, which passed through a pulley and had a weight on the end. You pulled the weight end of the rope to open the door. The wide stairs allowed the passage of incubators, apple cider barrels and sacks and sacks of freshly harvested potatoes.

The other entrance was and still is from inside of the house. Now since the front room has been converted into the kitchen, the entrance to the cellar is quite convenient. There is that narrow varnished door, with its equally very narrow steps, going down, down, down into the darkness of the cellar. Of course, since 1937 there is an electric bulb for illumination. But in the more ancient times of our childhood the trip to the cellar was quite an adventure.

There were no iceboxes, no refrigerators, no deep freezes. Mom bought very few canned foods in tin cans, outside of sardines and tuna fish. So trips to the cellar were frequent. Even the homemade bread was stored in a big white crock, covered with a simple white cotton dish towel.

We are eating supper. I am sitting at my assigned place at table on the bench, up against the wall, near the back corner of the kitchen.

"Ernie, get a loaf of bread!"

I slip under the table, crawl between all those legs, feet and knees, cross through the corner of the sitting room into the front room. I open the door to the front room, then the small wooden door to the cellar. On the log beam to the right there is a working flashlight. This is not so much a stairway; it is more like a ladder and the last step is sometimes missing. So I proceed with care.

Was I scared of the darkness of the cellar?

Who, me? Scared? I knew some scaredy-cat girls who would scream at seeing a big black spider, or worse, if their faces touched a spider web, they would come running out of the cellar screaming. But, golly gee, we boys were never scared, not of the cellar, nor of hoot owls, nor of swirling bats over the cedar trees in the orchard.

As one walked away from the ladder there was a medium-large cupboard to the right. This had Mason jars full of applesauce, beans, peas, beets and the like. Then in the southwest corner were the two big wooden bins full of potatoes. One bin held the early potatoes. Through daily family consumption, we emptied that bin around Christmas. The late potatoes were to hold us over until the new potatoes were dug up around the first week of August.

By March, the potatoes in the cellar began to sprout. Then there was that most unappealing job of cleaning the old potatoes of their new sprouts. But, of course, among every hundred potatoes there would be one or more rotten ones. There are few things as smelly and as icky as a thoroughly rotten potato. But the job must be done, because, like a bad apple, one rotten potato will spoil the lot.

The cellar floor was made of red bricks and the four walls with medium sized field stones, painted over with a thin coat of whitewash. The roof-ceiling had huge rough-hewn logs. All this, I presume, was constructed during the very earliest of the pioneer days.

All our farm buildings stand on a hill. The cellar has a small drainage tile which naturally drained towards the creek. We never had serious problems of water in the cellar. When the red bricks of the floor were well scrubbed and the walls recently whitewashed the cellar could be an inviting place.

Three sets of shelves were built directly into the brick walls, the tops forming an arc, like a niche in a church to receive a saint's statue. Over the years, other wooden shelves were added along the walls of the cellar. On the floor stood different sized crocks for sauerkraut, bread and pickles. There were barrels for apple cider, apple jack, and vinegar.

Sometimes we made root beer. The action of the yeast in the liquid was so strong that some bottles would explode. I've heard talk about homemade beer, but that is not a part of my personal experience.

In a sense, the cellar was what Thanksgiving Day is all about. It is a shame that we could not put on public display those rows of yellow peaches, red beets, green beans, sparkling strawberry jam, brown and white canned beef and the smells of sauerkraut, vinegar and apple cider.

On the south side of the cellar are two small barred windows, like ventilators, as outlets for air. During the summer, Mickey, the collie dog, would lie in front of these two windows, destroying all flowers, to take advantage of the cool air.

There was an old tale about a greedy wolf that got into a farmer's cellar by squeezing himself through some narrow window bars. In the cellar, the wolf ate so much that he grew too fat to escape through the window bars. I always imagined that wolf in our own cellar trying to get out of those little south windows.

Of course, there were no real wolves in our part of the country. Therefore, we pretty well celebrated Thanksgiving Day 365 days of the year, giving thanks to the Good Lord for all the goodies we had in our cellar. In spite of the occasional rotten potato, the black spiders and the scratchy, clawing itchy spider webs in our faces, the cellar was a genuine blessing.

In monastic orders, such as the Benedictines, the monk responsible for the over-all daily running of the monastery is called the Cellarer. He is not exactly the treasurer in charge of the accounting ledgers; he is not exactly responsible for maintenance; the Cellarer must see to it that there is daily food on the table. At our Precious Blood Brunnerdale Minor Seminary the priest responsible was called the Procurator but he served well as a Cellarer.

Whatever the Cellarer's duties in a monastery, I like the name/office/ title: Cellarer. Maybe a Cellarer was always a friendly ghost in our house. Our cellar was more than a place or a storeroom. There was a spirit there, a presence, a sense of bountiful goodness, a feeling of well being, of confidence, of thankfulness.

I like the idea that over the many generations we have nourished and entertained a friendly ghost under our house: the Cellarer.

31.
Christmas

The Ranly Christmas was so peculiar that we are almost embarrassed to talk about it. If the truth must be told, it was also largely non-religious. It was not secular in the sense of being over-commercialized. Our early Christmases were so very centered on Santa Claus.

When Mom understood what it meant to put Christ back into Christmas we got our first Nativity set. After that she was the first to bake a birthday cake for Baby Jesus and to have the grandchildren sing "Happy Birthday" in front of the Crib.

Christmas started with the feast of Saint Nicholas on the sixth of December. We had to write our letters to Santa Claus. We left the letters by our plates on the kitchen table. The concept of hanging up stockings on the fireplace struck us as very odd. With our natural gas we had no fireplace. (We knew no one who had a fireplace.) And why would someone hang out his old stinky stockings?

Saint Nick was true to his word. He picked up our letters overnight and left each of us a nice handful of candy as harbingers of better things to come. We knew all the traditional Christmas carols and the poem, "The Night before Christmas", which, of course, talked about hanging up stockings. What we sang day in and day out was, "I'm Dreaming of a White Christmas." What we lived intensely were the words from "Santa Claus Is Coming to Town." Paul brought the actual sheet music to the song which Teacher Eifert borrowed a few times for the school Christmas program in the C.K. of A. Hall.

With no effort I recall the words:

"You better watch out.
You better not cry.
You better not pout.
I'm telling you why.
Santa Claus is coming to town.
He sees you when you're sleeping.
He knows when you're awake.
He knows if you've been good or bad
So be good for goodness sake."

The Ranly Santa Claus was a combination of the wrathful judgment of God which at the last moment miraculously transformed Him into pure generosity to open up his sack full of gifts for us kids.

But first came the judgment. Sometime around the Feast of Saint Nick we woke up to find a packet of thin willow switches by the back porch. Santa Claus had brought them to keep us kids in line until Christmas.

This was a very silly thing, when I think about it. There was hardly any physical punishment in our family. This packet of switches was simply a threat which hung over our heads like the sword of Damocles. I never heard of the willow switches being used. They stood aside the cupboard behind the sitting room stove where we kept old shoes, and the switches were eventually burned in the same stove.

I remember the year we bought one green artificial wreath with a red electric bulb lighting up the yellow candle in the middle. This was hung in the south window of the sitting room. We could see the red light not only from the barn and from the hog stable, but walking home from town at night; passing by the cane press near the poplar tree we could see that red light like a beacon. It made us feel the spirit of Christmas.

Suddenly, one day the door to the porch room would be locked. That created a lot of excitement. Santa Claus was making preparations. In those days, Dad set up a tree there and only he and Mom (I suppose the older children) decorated the tree. Then when Santa Claus left on

Christmas Eve the fully decorated tree was moved to the front room. Yes, we used the front room at Christmas time.

The tree itself had its own tradition. Grandpa Ranly planted a windbreak of cedar trees along the north and east sides of the orchard. By my time, they were tall, ungainly trees. Every December, Dad sized up the trees and selected two well proportioned green branches. He sawed them off, brought them home and wired together the backs of the two branches. The result was a sort of Charlie Brown Christmas tree, but not so bad, really. And it was ours.

About this time, Mom decided that the whole family should help decorate the Christmas tree. I think for a year or so we may have bought a live tree. Later, Father Vic brought home a put-together artificial tree. So Christmas began to go modern.

Some Christmas tree decorations are family heirlooms. I am delighted that the Flaute family still cherishes a plastic pink Santa Claus and a little brown lion. We had small candles with tin clip candle holders, but we never lit the candles.

The first electric lights had us all oohing and aahing. But with that string of lights, if one little bulb was loose or burned out the whole set went out. Later a modest Nativity set was placed below the tree.

Santa Claus came live on Christmas Eve. We knew him best by the German word, Peltz Schnickel, which literally means "That Furry Fellow," "The Fellow in a Furry Suit." The coming of Pelz Schnickel was the major focus of weeks of talk and excitement.

Every year each of us, as corresponded to our age, had to learn by heart a new prayer, like "The Apostles Creed." You had to say it out loud and clear while Santa Claus was hovering over you with his whip. And he asked you if you had been good. He knew all about any recent high jinks we may have done. It was a miniature judgment of God that we awaited.

After all the chores were done on Christmas Eve we waited nervously in the house. Of a sudden, the windows rattled. There were knocks on all the doors. We heard the tingling of sleigh bells. In came Pelz Schnickel, dragging a leather strap of sleigh bells and a blacksnake whip.

Some years Santa came with a Helper. Then there was the threat of a black-suited Santa Claus who was known to be especially mean and strict. We huddled around Mom.

But as sure as the Christmas star itself, the transformation would take place. Santa would melt into pure heart. The big sack of toys was opened. We would be so excited over the new toys that we never noticed just when Santa Claus left. Once I did notice his back to us as he was taking a good drink of liquor. Well, he deserved it. He still had a long night's work ahead of him.

In those years, our pastor would announce: "Midnight Mass this year is at 6 a.m. in the morning." And so it was. Our parish had no tradition of Midnight Mass. We tried out all our new toys on Christmas Eve. We ate freshly baked Christmas cookies—stars and trees and Santa Clauses, covered with white sugar frosting and sprinkled with colored sugar.

We went to bed before midnight to be pulled from our beds at 5 a.m. in the dark cold of a winter's morning. Carols began at 5:30 with Dad singing first tenor in the choir loft and in his best days he played Silent Night on the violin. Did I say Silent Night? No. In those days it was Stille Nacht.

The dinner for Christmas was exceptional but within the immediate family. On good years there was enough snow to try out the new sleds. We were home from school until after New Year's, so we planned skating trips and went out to shoot sparrows with the new air rifle. We had afternoons free to play whole games of Monopoly, trying to win against the lucky player who had hotels on Park Place and Broadway.

On New Year's Eve the younger teenagers, even the girls, were coached into shooting a shotgun into the air from the front lawn. We kids ran around in circles with sparklers. By January 2 Mom and Dad were greatly relieved to send us off to school again.

None of my brothers and sisters retained these Christmas traditions for their own families. In fact, the very meanest of our Santa Clauses now said that Christmas is a feast of love and joy and not the fear of God which they themselves imposed upon us. I suppose it was for the good.

The Flaute family began to observe the four weeks of Advent as religiously as monks. Their children would be desperate because there were less than five days till Christmas and they still did not have a tree and all the other families had their trees and only the leftover scrubby trees would be on the lots for sale. But, no, the Twelve Days of Christmas begins on Christmas day itself.

During Advent, a Flaute girl spent a Saturday night in a friend's house. She returned home after the 10 a.m. Sunday High Mass. "Mom," she declared, in shock and disbelief. "That family does not have an Advent wreath!" She could not imagine Advent without a family Advent wreath.

So the new generations have new traditions. How nice. The way that the love of God is incarnated into our individual families, day by day and year by year, is always the work of the Spirit.

32.
Winter

Old folks always say that winters are not as cold as they used to be. I have little to say to that. I have no dramatic stories about exceptionally fierce winters. We read the poem "Snowbound" in school, but we never had the good (?) or bad (?) fortune to be severely snowbound. Simply, Ohio winters are a fact of life and we adapted ourselves accordingly.

For one thing, we had natural gas. The well was at the side of the road by the cane press and was owned cooperatively by something called the Cassella Gas Company. At one time the Company had numerous associates and extended as far south as the Gruenenwald Convent. But by my day, there were only a few families still actively connected by those ungainly steel half-inch gas pipes.

I am no geologist and I still have no idea how the whole operation worked. Every year (as I understand it) the well had to be "cleaned" in the sense that the water collected in the well had to be removed from the piping. So Dad and one of the Feltz boys would work all day at the well, becoming so covered with pitch and oil that they looked like real live black Santa Clauses—a very distinct reality in our family.

So we had a gas range in our kitchen that stayed lit day and night, winter and summer. On the coldest of mornings we all ran together, huddled around the stove, slowly pulling up our socks and putting on our shoes, while Mom was hovering over the stove, tending to the preparation of oatmeal for breakfast.

Sitting by an open fireplace on a cold winter night seems very romantic, picturesque; our scene was much more homey and down to earth. We sat around that gas range with our stockinged feet thrust into the open oven, shivering at the thought of running upstairs to bed.

There was a nightly row about who would go first to warm up the bed. The first one in bed under those heavy covers had to wait it out until simple body heat warmed up the first small area around the body. Then one slowly stretched out the legs to warm up a larger area.

I said "heavy covers." We accused Mom of confusing things. She was convinced that the answer was HEAVY blankets, but we insisted that heavy blankets were not necessarily WARM blankets.

The top mattress was a store-bought cotton thing, resting upon a straw-filled mattress on the bottom. Every summer right after threshing, all the upstairs bottom mattresses would be re-filled with fresh dry clean wheat straw. After a year of our tossing and turning and fighting in bed, the straw in the bottom mattress would be ground down to chaff and thrown out for bedding for the chickens in the chicken coop.

The stairs were in the middle of the house, with the Girls' Room to the right—to the south—and, past the middle room, the Boys' Room was to the left—to the north. At the head of the stairs was a small dish, a sugar bowl, I think, tied by a twine string to a nail in the wall by the door next to the Girls' Room. This was a Holy Water font.

Mom always had Holy Water in the house. We dutifully signed ourselves with Holy Water before going to bed at night and when we got up in the mornings. On really cold mornings as we stumbled out of bed we would find a layer of ice over the Holy Water. There was no central heating in those days.

I said we always had a fire in the gas range. On the very coldest days of winter, the gas line would freeze shut. That is, moisture condensed inside the steel pipes would turn into a liquid; this water would gather at a low spot in the pipe line. And when it was cold enough, the water would freeze so tight that no gas could pass.

This meant that the gas fixtures must be removed from the stove. A fire must be built with small kindling wood. A kettle full of water would be set to boil. Someone must take the boiling water, walk the pipe line, find the correct spot (like near the bridge) and pour the hot water at the exact spot of the pipe to melt the ice inside, freeing the gas to pass on to the house.

Mom would make oatmeal and coffee over the wood fire. Everyone would be in a bad mood. But the school children must be off because Teacher Eifert kept class records on school attendance and punctuality.

Our own creek was never very good for ice skating. The pond in the woods was also very small, but we made the best of it. Originally, we had only iron skates that had to be fitted upon the bottom of work shoes. From The Seminary we got some secondhand shoe skates.

Some winters dropped several feet of snow, but our farm had no really good hills for sledding. One winter with extraordinary snow we dared to sled down the almost perpendicular slopes of Lookout Mountain, the cut-away along the creek below Ashman's lane. Several times we lowered the big sleigh-surrey from the machine shed and with the small John Deere tractor took off down the lane on to the roads, riding the old black sleigh and singing Jingle Bells for all we could.

Our house was somewhat protected by the catalpa grove to the west. But driving west winds could leave deep drifts of snow from the garage to the barn. Also, the first fifty feet of the lane from the road would have high snow drifts from strong winds from either the south or the north. So there were days when no car could come and go and we could play at being snowbound.

Along with card games such as pinochle, euchre, sheepshead, war, gin rummy, we had table games such as monopoly, parcheesi and checkers. (The Ranlys never played bridge or chess.) Popcorn would be served. Better yet, we would bring in ice from the outside and make homemade ice cream. There was never a dull day even in the worst of winters.

Yet to see the first crocus peaking through the snow below the bridal wreath bush on the south side of the house was an occasion of great joy. Can spring be far behind?

33.
Magdalen

The word is pronounced with a long German AH. I thought the name came from a Great Aunt on my Mother's side, but Lucille says it was Grandma Speck's first name. Magdalen is the Ranly family name for playing house with paper cutouts.

I have the impression that our older sisters played Magdalen more than our generation. By my time it had become an established family tradition, along with our style of playing hide-and-seek which we called "wolf."

We used the family bible. Understand me well. We were a strict Roman Catholic family. We had the Baltimore Catechism with its three levels. We subscribed to the archdiocesan Catholic paper from Cincinnati. We had prayer books, Father Stedman's little Sunday Missals, Catholic calendars, holy cards, nineteenth century pictures of the Sacred Heart, a reproduction of da Vinci's Last Supper on the wall above the table in the kitchen; we had rosaries, medals, scapulars, holy water. But we did not have a copy of the Sacred Scriptures. Not even the New Testament.

By the family bible, I mean those two huge mail-order catalogues that arrived in late January/early February to help shake off the late winter blues. We received both of them, Monkey Wards and Sears and Sawbuck, as we called them. It was a great day when we found a new catalogue lying aside the mailbox at the end of the lane. We came puffing up the hill by the barn lugging a sparkling new catalogue. The new catalogue was carefully protected by Mom and the adults, but last year's immediately became the common property of all us kids.

The mail order catalogue was the backdrop for playing Magdalen. First, each player had to get a large piece of brown wrapping paper, that in which our catalogue purchases arrived by mail. The paper was smoothed out, turned over and marked off with our house of dreams, much like an architect's sketch of a one-story ranch house. In the catalogues we saw pictures of cutaway doll houses with all their miniature furniture, but that was a fantasy world for us. We were content to use brown wrapping paper to mark off the rooms, the doorways, the windows and perhaps sketch in where some of the major furniture would be placed.

And then began the more creative part. We had to make up, each of us, our own family. We did that by studying very carefully all the people pictured in the catalogue. This time, what sort of father do I want, one dressed in a business suit or in coveralls? And who would be my mother? How many children? What ages and what sex?

One by one, we made our selection and cut this year's family from the catalogue. We cut with great care, not only so that our own people would be prim and neat, but we were not to ruin too much of the catalogue because other kids had to cut out their choices.

Then we had to furnish the house, picking out colorful sofas, kitchen ranges, and ice boxes, the like of which we saw only in the houses of our city cousins.

We gave names to all the members of our family. Play would begin, say, when Father came home to eat, Mother had dinner ready, all the family sat around the table in the area designated as the kitchen. There would be family talk between all the cutouts.

Sometimes we created a real soap opera situation. We could play Magdalen alone, but usually it became a group game with several of us on the sitting room floor, looking over at the others to see how their family was doing. Sometimes, one whole family would come visiting another family. The possibilities were unlimited.

When play time was over, each of us carefully gathered together all the cutouts. We folded the brown paper inwards so that all the figures were safely protected and then we guarded the little package in a secret place.

The next time we could create an altogether new chapter in the unending saga of Magdalen.

A boy could play Magdalen, retaining his machismo, until about the age of eight. Under the pretext of playing with her baby sister, a girl could play until the early teens. It was a good substitute for not reading LITTLE WOMEN.

I think our family could have taken Harry Potter in stride. We knew people in minor seminaries and aspirancies and so could relate to boarding school experiences. (My own minor seminary matched Hogswart in some matters.) We had some friendly family ghosts, but our German Catholic culture taught us that there is a touch of evil in HEXEREI—witchcraft. No fooling around here.

Magdalen allowed creativity. We made up each family from scratch. Ours was a family setting, free from monsters and cosmic conflicts. Playing doctors-and-nurses, or playing school (which with us was popular) or acting out live theater gave each child a specific role. Magdalen had us act out each role in a given family in their various complex relationships.

I wonder now if we unconsciously acted out our personal life dramas in playing Magdalen. Thank God, no family therapist observed us.

I see something inherently healthy in all this. We had no TV, not the violence of cartoons nor the good shows such as Kaptain Kangaroo and Sesame Street. I think we gained self-identity and self-confidence without becoming insolent or overbearing.

By definition, Magdalen was active. No one could remain passive, indifferent, aloof from life when playing Magdalen.

Sometimes I think we should market our family game of Magdalen, like hula hoops or Pokémon. But that is a contradiction. The very essence of Magdalen (and all good family games) is that it is spontaneous and, in the strict sense, unique. Every family has its own genius and that genius must be cultivated in its own special way.

34.
Hunting Eggs

We had around two hundred laying hens, white leghorns, and a few gray heavies thrown in so that we always found a few brown eggs among all the white ones. The L-shaped chicken house behind the pear trees was expanded once so that the chickens had more space to roost at night.

Cleaning the chicken house was a stinky job but it had to be done about every three months. The green, asbestos-shingled brooder house used to be in the orchard behind the bee stable. I never did like the brooder house when it sat in the three-acre field in front of the house.

We did not gather eggs: we hunted eggs. This was done twice a day, before dinner and in the late afternoon. There were more eggs in the morning than later in the day. The rows of nests/boxes were along the west wall.

If a hen was actually sitting on the nest, you had to be careful to slip your hands slowly under the hen and pull out from under her all the warm, white eggs, without disturbing her in her process of dropping an egg. If a hen was "clucking" we had to tell Mom and she put that hen in a separate cage for a few days.

Always a few hens laid their eggs on the very floor of the coop. So we walked carefully to find the eggs. We walked carefully for other reasons, too. Fresh chicken dropping are hard to clean off your shoes and what they do to bare feet is not fit to put into words.

The windows of the chicken house looked south and east so that sunshine poured into the house throughout the morning hours. On a cold winter morning there was nothing better to warm the human heart than to step into the chicken house. The sunlight reflected off the white feathers of the hens as they ate ground grain from the wooden feeders on the floor or drank at the water fountains, each one tipping up its head at every drop of water. There was the music of peace and contentment, a hundred or more clucking, cooing hens. And a few soloists, those hens who had just dropped a sticky hot egg in the nest and came out to sing to high heaven about the achievement. There is no better cry of joy, no better praise of life than the alleluia of a cackling hen who has just deposited an egg.

During the cold of the winter the layers remained closed up in the chicken house. But by early spring the chicken house door was opened around midday so that after laying their daily egg, the hens could feed upon the fresh grass and scratch for earth worms outside. At dusk, the chickens simply came home to roost and one of us kids had to close the chicken house door for the night. It was a bad start of a day when we got up in the morning to find the chickens out. Someone had forgotten to close the chicken house door.

I still remember the incubators. They were stored above the smoke house. Around March they were taken down, repaired and then set up in the cellar. The eggs were spread out, and a live flame from the kerosene burner kept them at a consistent warm temperature.

There came a time when the eggs had to be candled. I didn't understand much about that but it seemed some eggs were thrown out because they had not produced a living embryo.

Then came the magic moment. An egg would crack from within. A small hole would appear. Then a head would stick out with two beady eyes and a bill pecking at the shell of the egg. The shell would fall apart and there sat a damp, shivering, fully developed chick. In a short time the chick would stand, move its wings and move about. As it dried, its color became a creamy yellow, like a soft dandelion flower. In another short time it began picking at food. No wonder new born chicks and Easter Eggs are signs of new life and of resurrection.

Meanwhile the brooder house had been prepared. The brooder apparatus hung all year from the inside roof. It was taken down, cleaned, tested. The whole thing was a round tin tent which set on the floor like a large toadstool. Underneath the hood was a kerosene burner which maintained the temperature at the level of the body heat of the chicks. Or, it would be better to say, at the level of the body heat of a mother hen. The few hundred chirping chicks made a low sweet sound .

We must have given up the use of incubators by 1938. After that we bought day-old chicks directly from the hatchery. I seem to remember that one year the mailman dropped two flat cardboard boxes of live chicks. We brought the boxes of live chicks directly into the warm, cleaned, prepared brooder house.

Far too quickly for us, the chicks lost their original beauty and then large coarse white feathers would replace the yellow down. At about two months, a new beauty arrived when the whole flock would be perfectly white. The combs would become more pronounced and we began to distinguish which ones were the roosters.

By the Fourth of July the roosters would be sold as fryers. We caught them by spreading cracked corn over the ground. We had a long heavy wire with an open hook at the end. With this we snatched the roosters one by one as they gathered to eat the cracked corn. For our own eating, it was only a matter of hours to catch, clean and dress a few fryers. Then there we were around the kitchen table, eating fried spring chicken, along with mashed potatoes and gravy.

Once a city cousin watched us cut the heads off of chickens and he never ate chicken again. Well, life is cruel, but at least on the farm we faced up to the full reality.

We had a cutting block behind the woodshed made from one of the tree-beams from the new barn. One kid held the legs and wings; another stretched out the head over the wooden block. Hopefully, mercifully, there would be only one blow with the axe.

It is best to hold on to the wings and feet until all the blood drained out and the chicken came to a peaceful rest. But if the wings got loose and fluttered into the flowing blood, well, things got pretty messy. Better not describe the whole scene. We understood well the expression: "He ran around like a chicken with its head cut off."

Then a bucket of hot scalding water came from the kitchen. Each bird, one by one, was stuck into the bucket and squished about until the very roots of all the feathers were soaked through and through. We plucked out the feathers rapidly because the feathers pulled best when the whole mess was still hot and sticky. Most of the pin feathers came out on the first pull. A freshly plucked, clean chicken can be an exhibit of great skill.

In the house, Mom would hold each chicken over the blue flame of a gas burner to singe off the body hair. This made a blue, acrid smelling smoke, almost like church incense. Our "Ohio fried chicken" was rolled in flour with salt and pepper and fried in a heavy iron skillet.

Towards the end of August we began finding little white eggs in and around the brooder house. Our sweet little golden chicks had become pullets and now were about to grow into layers. That meant they must be transferred from the brooder house to the chicken house.

For some weeks already many of the pullets were roosting, sleeping nights in the trees in the orchard. Carrying chickens was an all-family job. Even a five-year old was big enough to carry two chickens, one in each hand.

We started in the brooder house. The big people picked the sleeping pullets off the roost and handed them to us smaller kids. We would carry two or three in each hand, walk then over to the chicken house, drop them on the floor and close the door on them. This involved quite a few trips.

When we emptied the brooder house, the real fun began. Now someone had to snatch the pullets sleeping on the tree boughs. Some were so low that we could reach them from the ground, especially those in the old cedar trees. But for others, someone had to climb a tree, crawl out on the branches and hand the chickens down to us on the ground.

Of course, one or the other pullet would wake up and, with a start, fly off. The next day and night we scoured the orchard to see how many chickens had escaped us. After dark, we chased them down, one by one. Catching and carrying chickens was a once-a-year job. For us, once a year was one time too many.

We kept only a few roosters. I do not have memories of waking up to the crowing of roosters. Once in a while, a laying hen would get away from us, lay a nest of eggs secretly in some corner of the barn and then suddenly appear with a brood of little chicks to itself. Mom would feign disappointment or resentment, but she loved the antics of a mother hen with its chicks as much as we did.

As a special project we usually had a small number of brightly colored bantam fowl which we called bandies. They largely had to survive on their own, lay and hatch their own young, protect them and grub around for food on their own. Bandies added life and color to the farmyard.

Then we had about a dozen or more guinea fowl, dark gray creatures, spotted with white, with a kind of turkey head. They roosted in the cedar tree by the hog lane where they served as sentries, making a great scrabble of noises at night if anything big moved near them. They hid their eggs any and everywhere so that in their case we literally had to hunt for guinea eggs. Some times we found their nests with as many as twenty or more eggs, nests as far away as the hedge fence along the creek. With so many eggs on hand for family consumption Mom would bake angel food cake.

We kept the eggs in the smoke house. The egg man came once a week. We had to clean the eggs with a damp cloth or with a soft sandpaper brush. Then we boxed the eggs, layer by layer, in special paper cartons. Cracked and broken eggs were set aside and carried to the kitchen.

Feeding and caring for the chickens and eggs was largely the task for women. Mom was the overseer. And she loved it. As she neared the chicken house with a bucket of shelled corn the chickens crowded about her like the multitudes around Jesus. We have a black and white home movie of Father Vic's that shows Mom with her chickens. My favorite has her holding up her big apron full of the eggs she had just gathered from the chicken house.

Today the egg business is big business. So be it. Too bad there is not a place in it for Mom with her apron full of eggs.

35.
Butchering

You slaughter cattle and steers, but you butcher hogs. A steer could be slaughtered in spring or fall; butchering must be done in the dead cold of winter.

Slaughtering a steer was a relatively easy task. It was done simply within the context of the family itself.

Once the steer was lying dead on the ground, the hide was cut off, a single tree was set between the back legs, and then the carcass was hoisted up by a block and tackle. The enormous ball of intestines was removed and then someone went to work with a meat saw to cut the backbone exactly down the middle so that all the T-bone steaks would be even and square. Then the carcass was cut into four quarters and each one hauled off to be divided up according to the cuts preferred: round steaks, standing rib roast, sirloins and so on. Someone went through the intestines to recover the heart, the liver, the kidneys. But this was all relatively easy and quick.

Butchering hogs was a major event. As we said, it was done only in the dead of winter, because nature's cold was essential to cool and preserve the meat.

Butchering was a social event. Family and relatives are one set of social life; butchering neighbors were a completely different set. Threshing neighbors were a larger, more distant group. Butchering neighbors comprised a small group of near neighbors who almost became closer than uncles/aunts/cousins. At all major moments— serious sickness, death, weddings—butchering neighbors automatically show up at your door with plates of sandwiches, a kettle of soup, a freshly baked cake and they ask: How can we help?

The hogs to be butchered had been selected months before. The preferred market weight was 210-220 pounds, but butchering hogs were much larger, even up to 300 pounds or more. Dad was up hours before daylight to have a roaring fire burning under the big iron water kettle. The regular chores—milking cows, feeding the chickens, slopping the hogs—had to be done, but today there is a special sense of excitement in the air. Neighbors arrive, the women go directly to the house, the men stand around, asking how they can help. We eat the oatmeal breakfast hurriedly with the hope we can witness the first blows. But, of course, our school buckets are prepared and sooner or later we will have to rush off to school.

To describe what follows may seem cruel, heartless, but it was not that way at all. The man with the .22 caliber rifle took careful aim at a spot between the eyes of each hog. The animal fell with a short grunt. A sharp knife found the jugular vein and every last drop of blood was pumped out of the warm body into a bucket. A second pig was felled. The steamy red gurgling blood was gathered and poured into a common bucket, where someone was constantly stirring the blood. There was a third hog, maybe a fourth; five in one day was unusual. Someone took the blood to the house, still stirring. There the women took charge to oversee the proper curdling and cooling of the blood.

The hot boiling water Dad had prepared in the big iron kettle was poured into the wooden scalding barrel, along with ashes from the wood fire. The first hog was dragged to the cleaning area, a rope tied to its hind legs, and by a hoist and pulley it was lifted above the barrel. Then it was slowly lowered into the steaming barrel. There was a swooshing and pooshing of the hog inside the barrel. Experts pulled at the hog's hairs, testing to see if they pulled out on touch. The carcass dare not stay in the hot water too long. Finally, someone declared that the hair and skin were ripe. The hog was hoisted up out of the barrel and laid out on what we called the butchering table. This was two pieces of solid iron with a grid of holes one inch square, so that water and grime could fall through.

The whole crew of men fell upon the carcass like vultures, tearing at the hair and scraping at the skin with serrated tin blades. The pure white skin began to shine through all the dirt and grime and the hair. Some perfectionist always wanted it cleaner, but the pragmatists would holler: "Bring on another hog!"

Hot water was added to the scalding barrel. The rope was transferred to the second hog and the process repeated. What a sight to see three/four white carcasses lying on the two wheeled trailer.

Gutting a pig is really quite simple. Very few parts go to waste. Will we use the stomach and the large intestines for blood pudding? Of course, all the small intestines are extracted, their contents thrown away. Later, one by one, each thin slimy snake of an intestine must be scraped clean with a table knife. And there you have your sausage casings.

Just how all the processes went from scraping clean the carcass to the final pork products I cannot tell you in detail because, of course, I was in school until 4 p.m. Coming home from school, we kids snuck into the house with all the expectations of Christmas Eve. We found Mom with the neighbor women, their deft hands moving as fast as their lips, as they worked, talked and laughed through the late afternoon.

I would sneak into the cool of Mom and Dad's bedroom where the cakes and pies, left over from dinner, were stored, waiting to be served for supper. Mom wouldn't miss a little slice of pie here, a small piece of cake, a smudge of a cake's icing.

By this time of the day the kettle of blood pudding was boiling mightily. We found pieces of the heart and tongue, cut off slices, salted them, and then chewed them like chewing gum. All the fat and gristle were boiling, changing colors from white to dull brown. This is called rendering lard. To this day I still do not understand why those strange words: to render lard.

Best of all, the sausage meat was being ground. We watched the pink/white meat fall into a big wooden tub that during the rest of the year was our wash tub—laundry tub. The experts came to season the sausage, pouring in little tins of black pepper along with handfuls of white salt.

Then one must mix and stir and turn and twist the meat, like kneading bread dough, in order to distribute evenly the condiments throughout the whole mass of meat.

Stuffing sausage was the work of two people, accompanied by a sympathetic crowd watching on the sidelines. The sausage stuffer was an ingenious invention. The lid on the black bowl was swung off to the side. With bare hands the soft, slippery meat was scooped into the sausage stuffer. The lid was set. Meanwhile, the other operator has slipped a long, sloppy casing on the spout of the machine.

Now came the moment of perfect coordination. The one in front sits with a large shallow pan on his lap, like the drip pan we used in washing and drying dishes. The person at the spout must have a firm grip on the very end of the casing so that the first spurt of sausage coming out of the spout is not a surprise. Then the second person cautiously turns the handle of the sausage stuffer, watching the meat squeeze in and around the descending lid.

And then it begins. The meat comes spurting out of the spout, filling up the casing, which systematically slips off the spout. With care, the sausage is guided to form a small spiral and then always a larger widening spiral with the hope that there would be no break in the whole casing. It was a real feat to empty all the ground meat of the full stuffer into one long casing.

Many other operations are going on at the same time. The blood pudding is being put away, stuffed into large intestines and stomachs. The lard is declared finished. This means that the hot liquid must be scooped out of the kettle and put into a pan-like sieve lined with a thin cotton cloth like a strainer. The hot grease passes through and falls into three-gallon tin lard cans. The cloth, like a sack, catches the pieces of skin and meat. This, in turn, is squeezed to get out the last possible drop of lard. What is left in the cloth-sack are brown pieces of skin and meat, which are called cracklings.

While the cracklings are still hot, you add salt and eat them like popcorn. I know, at bars you can buy little cellophane bags which are called "cracklings." But these store bought things are not even a shadow of what the real things are like. Hot, fresh, salted cracklings taste like butchering days.

I've barely mentioned the meat grinder. This was a mechanical masterpiece, about as interesting as the sausage stuffer. One needed a degree in mechanical engineering to assemble a meat grinder.

Fasten the meat grinder tight to the side of a wooden table with screw clamps on the bottom. Slip in carefully the grooved piston-like rod with its handle. Decide the coarseness of the ground meat by choosing between several sizes of holes. But first slip in the knife, then the metal piece with the small holes, then a washer and then a specially fitted screw. All snugly fit, but not too tight.

One turned the handle like cranking an old car. Small pieces of boneless meat were dropped into the open top of the grinder. The meat slid along the grooved shaft until it was forced up against the razor-sharp blade. The meat ground and fine now poured out the front from all those small metal holes.

Grinding sausage meat was fascinating to watch and fun to operate— the first ten minutes. It quickly became work, feeding the grinder and turning the handle.

To conclude the story on butchering I will violate again the rules I set up for myself. What I tell here is not my story; it happened after I left home. But it is a piece of priceless family lore which not even Ripley would have believed.

It was butchering day at the Ranlys. Mechanization had arrived. An electric motor now operated the meat grinder. The task of grinding the sausage was finished. My brothers began to take apart the meat grinder for washing. My little brother Don was examining the working end, trying to understand how the knife worked on that circular shaft. My brother Orville was removing the belt from the electric motor and thoughtlessly gave the flywheel a whirl. This force was strong enough to set into motion the whole mechanical chain and the knife blade made its motion and cut off a sizable tip of the forefinger on Don's right hand.

Well, accidents will happen. This was a piece of bad luck, especially sad, because Orville always felt somehow responsible.

A year later. It was butchering day at the Ranlys. The sausage meat is all ground. My same brother Don is at the same end of the machine. He is curious. How was it possible, he says to himself, that last year I stuck this finger in here by this blade and then, when the shaft turned...and he cut a piece off his middle finger on the same hand.

This is a true story.

You can look it up in the record books.

Or check out Don's finger.

36.
Kempers

Grandpa and Grandma Kemper, with an old maid daughter Maggie, lived in a little green house under a few cedar trees on the other side of the road to the left of the end of the lane. They had a big vegetable garden, one milk cow and an acre or more of land.

Grandpa Kemper had a long white beard, like Santa Claus. He grew his own tobacco and smoked a long-stemmed pipe. Of a quiet fall morning, when Grandpa Kemper walked ahead of us on the road, he on his way to the 8 a.m. Mass, we on our way to school, we could smell the smoke, puff by puff, as it wafted past us.

I try to remember Grandma Kemper, but I cannot distinguish her well from Maggie. It was Grandma who lay in the coffin when Mom took me by the hand and talked to me in reassuring terms about the mystery of death. I remember a blanket/shawl covered her feet and that she wore no shoes.

Old maid is an unmarried woman who passes a certain age when she is universally considered as unmarriageable. In many cultures, this happens to the last surviving daughter of a family who then is expected to care for her parents in their old age. In the case of the Kempers, for reasons unknown to me Maggie was simply an old maid.

We have the case of our cousin Lorrain Lamm, who, because she was the last child, was for all her life the Baby, never married, and, still living at ninety, has the name Babe. Old maid is not necessarily a term of disrespect or ridicule. Cousin Babe and Maggie Kemper are prize models of old maids, loving and lovable.

Although my memory of Grandma Kemper is very vague, she plays a major role in my life. In the Latino culture, she would be my "co-mother" or possibly a God Mother. You see, Grandma Kemper was midwife to Mom at the moment of my birth.

This was during the late morning hours of February 19, 1930.

That year spring came early to Ohio. New fresh dandelion greens were gathered, washed and served as salad with vinegar and bits of fried bacon. It was so warm that Grandma Kemper slipped out of that little green house and walked up our long lane without a winter coat.

How do I know? Well, I was there. I was delivered a tiny baby, the twelfth birth of sixteen for Mom.

Of course, it was Mom who so often told me all these details and what it was like that morning. I feel that I can talk about that day in the first person singular.

On the other hand, I marvel at Mom. As Saint Luke says in his Gospel, Mary, the Mother of Jesus, "kept all these things in her heart." How could Mom remember and recount the details of sixteen births?

What happened to the Kempers I do not understand well, because I was no longer living at home. In time the three Kempers I knew passed away. Their young Grandson, Florian Rosengarten, whom they had taken in as their own after he lost his mother, married and lived in the house for several years before it was sold to a new family.

What made all this so special is that the family was non-Catholic in an area where a hundred percent of the population was German Catholic. When the oldest boy of the family became of age, the parents consented to have him receive Catholic instructions, so that in time he was baptized. On his own, he set an admirable example of fidelity to all church services.

The family was very poor and eventually moved away, and the house, the garden, the trees were abandoned. Somewhere there must have been a legal transfer of title of the land to a neighboring farmer.

One summer afternoon the Chickasaw fire department scheduled a fire drill for its volunteers. They torched the Kemper house, and the firemen—there were no fire women in those days—practiced hosing down the flames and some rescue techniques. Then the trees were felled and the whole area bulldozed and leveled so that it was swallowed up into one big cultivated field. Now no one can tell where the house once stood. No one can tell that there ever was a place and a family called the Kempers.

This kind of disappearance or absence is more than a vacuum. It is more like a black hole that swallows up the whole past. Those of our generation try to remember the house and the family. But I feel sad, eerie, wistful, almost fatalistic when I see how a whole family, a way of life, can disappear and not leave a trace.

Physically, not leave a trace.

37.
Milking

Our city cousins from Dayton were fascinated to see how milk came from cows. This was no mystery to us. The fascination disappeared quickly enough if one had to get himself out of bed on a cold winter morning and milk two or more cows before breakfast and then off to school for the day.

But worse was milking cows on a hot sultry summer evening, the sides of the cows heaving with the heat, and the tails, caked with mud and with things much worse than mud, swatting at flies with the force of a whip.

Milking cows synthesized the worst and the best of our lives.

For one thing, there was the discipline involved. The cows must be milked, morning and evening, every day of the year, come hell or high water, Christmas, First Communion, butchering, threshing or what have you. I am not saying that the discipline was bad. It was simply an unchanging fact of life.

Milking cows could be a dirty, messy job. While the new barn had stanchions, we milked the cows in their own stable. However much we bedded them down with loose, clean straw from the straw stack or with shredded corn fodder, cows do what they must do and they can make themselves very dirty. A bucket of water and a damp cloth helps, but milking can be a messy job.

During the summer we bought liquid fly killer in gallon tin cans. Before milking, we sprayed the back ends of the cows to hold off the swarming flies. But that was no guarantee that a matted, dirty tail would not swat you in the face so hard it made the tears fall.

Yet milk cows are dear, lovable creatures. Each one had its name, each its distinct character. One was an easy milker, another a hard milker, and that one over there is a kicker. Take care with a kicker. Usually, only the big people milked the kickers.

I never remember having our own bull. Dad bought into the system of artificial insemination very early. This meant that we were to watch closely when a cow was "bullying"—was in heat—and a technician came—he was not exactly a veterinary—to perform that most unsavory task of artificial insemination.

The milk of a pregnant cow goes dry some three months before a new birthing. So it was not milked during this time. A new calf was an event of great importance. Usually the calving occurred over night. But a daytime birth was a spectacle of great wonder.

We never had pure breed stock, but there was a good sense of the quality of the mother cow and the chosen semen to help select the new heifers to be included into the milking herd. If a new calf was to be marketed, it was sold within a week and the mother cow, with now an ample supply of milk, would increase our sale of milk. If a calf was to be saved, it was weaned from its mother in a week or so. Pity the poor mother cow: estranged from its newborn calf, it would moo disconsolately for days and try to find its offspring within the barn.

Then we had to feed the young calf with a bucket half-full of milk diluted with water. We had to teach the calf how to drink.

You did that by sticking your fingers into the calf's mouth. Instinctively, the calf sucked your hand and licked it compulsively with its rough tongue. Then you guided the head of the calf into the bucket and the sucking action of the calf would have it take in quantities of milk. With feeding twice a day, in a week or so the calf would learn to drink from a bucket by itself without the need of your fingers. And slowly it would begin to munch upon alfalfa and ground grain.

Now as kids, we knew the difference between girl calves and boy calves and we knew what happened to those who went to market. Boy calves became steers, but just how that happened we were not sure. When we ate roast beef through the long months of winter we well remembered last year's prize steer which we had watched being butchered. Sentimentality could not deter us from the basic needs of life.

A girl calf became a heifer and eventually had its own first calf. To begin milking a new heifer mother required tact, patience, love and, at times, rather severe discipline. But over the months and the years the cow became a well balanced, integrated member of our milking herd.

Much of our romance with cows was leading them out to pasture and then driving them home at milking time. Our collie, Mickey, along with a smaller dog (my favorite was Jenny) were not the expert herding dogs of the movies, but they had a good sense of retrieving some runaway heifers and driving along a whole herd from behind. Of course, the cows were quite cooperative to our calls because they were coming home to the barn for water, for feeding (especially ground grain) and for the relief of being milked.

By early June, the cows were also let out to pasture over night. That meant that at the moment of the first sun in the morning someone (and a young lad like myself was very much indicated) must get the cows to the barn for the morning milking.

Maybe I groused about the moment Mom called up the stairs: "Time to get up!" But now I look upon those early summer mornings as treasured moments of intimacy and love with nature. Besides the orchard and the woods, we had eight separate fields, all with fences, so that, by rotating farming, the designated cow pasture for any year could be as far away as the field behind the woods by the Stelzer's line fence or as close as the field directly behind the barn.

Early in the spring, with all the rains, the pastures were so soft the cows would trample down the tender clover into the mud. Yet last winter's supply of loose hay in the mow was pretty well depleted. So the cows were pastured along the two sides of the road where the blue grass was tall and verdant from the spring rains. (This was before the county began clipping the grass along the roads.)

Our task was to watch cows. As the cows came upon the road and turned to go to town, we had to get ahead of them and wait for them at the big poplar tree near the Feltz fence line. There we turned them around and walked ahead of them up to Ashman's hill. It was an easy job; we were outside on beautiful early summer days.

But we always complained about watching cows. I don't know why we didn't enjoy more the wind rustling the leaves of the poplar tree, sending pollen blowing across the road like loose snow. Watching cows was a task only for early summer days.

Every cow was marked by the quantity of milk and its cream content. The milkman tested our milk every month and the price we received depended upon the percentage of cream in the milk. We had a very sophisticated cream separator which, through the action of centrifugal motion, separated the skim milk from the cream. But in my day, we no longer used the milk separator.

I saw butter churns at fairs. I knew how they worked. But in my time at home we did not make our own butter. Oh, I remember when someone might fill up a small tin can with milk and shake it steadily until, mysteriously, some butter would harden and then we drank the remaining buttermilk.

As a matter of fact, we ate very little butter. Mom bought oleo; now it is called margarine. There were laws against selling yellow oleo for fear it would be taken as butter. So with every bar of oleo there was a small packet of yellow food coloring. The girls took the soft oleo, added the powdered coloring and kneaded the mass as if it were bread dough until the whole mass was an even yellow color. And it was this that we spread on homemade bread.

Selling milk involved another chain of activities. Every morning the milk truck drove up the lane, rumbled across the bridge, turned up towards the house and then backed up to the water tank under the wind pump.

The milkman, along with the mailman, served as a link for social communication. Everyone, all the time, talked about the weather; but the milkman might carry news about a sick neighbor, about impassable roads in winter.

There were years when the same milkman served us and Walt and Alvina beyond Guadalupe. The milkman graciously consented to take one or two of us kids into his cab and drop us off at our destination.

I learned to have great respect for the honesty and the hard work of the milkman. He had to pull the steel cans, full of milk, out of tanks and coolers and throw them up upon the truck. The cans were all marked with numbers and each had its place on the truck. In time, I was able to climb the truck and I knew the numbers to hand down the empty cans. The same milkman delivered the milk check every two weeks, which Mom used to buy clothes and groceries.

We usually sold two cans of milk daily. Before the evening milking, someone had to wash out the metal milk cans and bring from the house the milk strainer along with round pads of white gauze. This gauze fit at the bottom of the strainer which had the shape of a large funnel. The milkers poured the fresh warm foamy milk, bucket by bucket, into the strainer and then the milk fell into the can. Only when the milk can was almost full did a stronger person lift the can into the tank full of cool water. If the cans were still half empty, they would float and tip over in the water of the tank.

When all the cows were milked, the strainer was taken off and the lids securely closed upon the milk cans. The pad was removed from the strainer and thrown to the cats and dogs. The cats licked at it gingerly, but Mickey, the collie, swallowed the whole thing in one gulp. I wondered about the dog's digestive system. Finally, the milk buckets were rinsed out with clean water and set upon a beam next to the barn in readiness for next morning's milking.

During the hottest days there was danger that the milk would sour overnight and be rejected by the milk plant. In that case, it would be returned the following day and we ate tons of cottage cheese for a few days. In the winter, the full milk cans stayed in the barn over night with the expectation that the animal warmth would stave off freezing.

During my high school days at the minor seminary I received my highest grade in English composition on the essay I wrote about our cows' names. To begin with, Mom and Dad would not permit saints' names for animals. That was somehow sacrilegious. Some names were obvious: Zebra, Reddy, Blacky; then there was Lady. The naming took place when a calf was being weaned from its mother cow.

But for one particular heifer, we lost our creativity. No one came up with a winning name. In the interval, it was called No Name. Finally, we were milking No Name. And the name stuck. I concluded my essay: To what lengths will a family go to name its cows. To have a cow with the stupid name of No Name.

38.
Lent and Holy Week

That big black blotch of ashes on the forehead was not to be washed off. The Ash Wednesday Mass was something very special; it was not just the ordinary 8 a.m. Mass with which we began every school day. The church was full, like a Sunday Mass. Mothers brought toddlers and babes in arms. Although the priest's admonition was solemnly proclaimed in Latin, we knew that we were dust and into dust we shall return. I often wondered why little children and babies needed this reminder of our common mortality.

Everyone took Lent seriously. For adults, this meant fasting, eating meat only once a day, not eating between meals and what was consumed at breakfast and lunch not exceeding the one big meal. That Fridays were meatless was simply a fact of life all year round.

For us children, Lent meant not eating candy.

To begin with, we never had much candy. When Mom sent us to the Dahlinghaus store for bologna or for some little thing like Fleischmann's yeast, Mary Dahlinghaus would invite us to choose some penny candy from behind the glass showcase. The decision was often difficult in the face of so many choices: an all-day sucker, chocolate covered marshmallows, kisses wrapped in silver foil with a white pull-string at the top, a "baseball bat" which was a long narrow taffy attached to a stick, or simply hard tack. Candy was our reward for the half-mile walk to town and then the half-mile walk back home again. We never complained to be asked to go to the store. But before we left, Mom would look us over to see if we were presentable to the better half of society: the townspeople.

But now it is Lent. We politely thank Mrs. Dahlinghaus, take the candy and guard it carefully in some secret pocket. At home, each of us has a special place to keep and hide the candy during the forty days of Lent. An old tin cookie box makes an excellent receptacle.

Surprisingly, the box will slowly fill up. There would be candy from visiting aunts, from older sisters who work away from home. But the treasure grows. At times we open our boxes, count the pieces and try to savor what each piece of candy will taste like on Holy Saturday.

I remember visiting our cousins, the Reicherts of Coldwater, and it happened to be Lent. Aunt Cora, always the thoughtful hostess, made chocolate fudge for us, her guests, and for her family.

To us, chocolate fudge was candy. This was a real case of conscience. What do we do? We slyly slunk behind Mom and she immediately intuited our dilemma. Without ado she left us to understand that politeness and charity were more important than the rule against eating candy during Lent. The great moral theologian, Saint Alphonse Liguori, could not improve that advice. To say that we enjoyed eating that chocolate fudge without scruple is an understatement.

For those meatless meals during Lent Mom and Dad (and other adults) ate pickled herring. At first the very smell of the vinegar/brine and the touch of cold raw fish were repellent to me. But by the age of ten I began to cherish this food which came out of small wooden buckets.

I began to see that Lent really was not all that bad. It was not so much penance as a nice variation in diet and perhaps much more healthy food for all concerned. Mom and Dad ate their pickled herring on soda crackers with great gusto.

There is a lot of propaganda about the Family Rosary. "The family that prays together, stays together." I have the impression that before my time there was more praying of the Family Rosary. I do not know.

Lent was the time for saying the Rosary together. Around 8 at night, we all got up from our chairs, turned around, knelt directly in front of the chair we had been sitting on, slumped down over the chair and began mumbling Our Fathers and Hail Marys. The leader had a Rosary; the rest of us had our ten fingers. The little ones would fall asleep.

By the time of the Marian litany, the mumbling was reduced to a low hum, almost a groan. Our Lord had his agonized prayer in the Garden of Olives, but this common family agony, spread all over the kitchen and the sitting room, was not exactly inspirational prayer. Over the years, not even Mom could hold herself or us to the discipline of a daily family Rosary during Lent.

The 7:30 a.m. Mass every Sunday was a Low Mass; the 10 a.m. o'clock High Mass was preceded by the saying of the Rosary. The men's choir sang all the sung parts in Latin from the choir loft. All year long we had church on Sunday afternoons at 2 p.m.

Please note: church is a building. But when we go to church for services, WE HAVE CHURCH. As I was saying, we had church every Sunday afternoon, concluding with Benediction of the Blessed Sacrament.

During Lent, Sunday afternoon church included the fourteen stations of the Way of the Cross. As Mass servers—we never knew the word ACOLYTE—we boys accompanied the priest up and down the center aisle, opposite those fourteen milk-colored statues on pedestals standing away from the walls. It was always sort of dramatic, this story in fourteen acts that ended with Jesus dead and buried. It was only after the Second Vatican Council that many groups added the fifteenth station: The Resurrection of Jesus. With the Resurrection, the whole story is, indeed, very dramatic.

Following the Liturgical Calendar of the time, the Sunday before Palm Sunday was Passion Sunday and all the statues in church were covered with purple cloth. Then on Palm Sunday during the Mass itself, while the priest mumbled a reading in Latin, Teacher Eifert read the whole Passion story from the choir loft in English.

We brought our blessed palms home, but we were not all that skilled at braiding palms. Mom made little crosses out of two pieces of palm and we put them in all the buildings—the barn, the hog stable, the chicken house, the machine shed—for God's blessings and protection.

The rest of the blessed palms were stored alongside some candles that had been blessed on February 2, Candlemas Day. These were to be used throughout the year to fend off all dangers from wind, rain, thunder and lightning.

To this day I can still sense the smell of burnt palm when lightning strikes close. I think all my sisters carried this custom to their own families. During threatening storms, Mom lit a candle and then, prayerfully and trembling, burned palms over the fluttering flame. It makes a pleasant acrid smell, almost like incense.

I've heard it said that it was a scientific fact the palm smoke of itself repelled lightning. I have no data on that. But the tin roofs could roll and rumble in the wind, the chinese elm in front of the sitting room would have its branches rent and torn, thunder could crack all around us, but no lightning ever struck our place while we were praying with burnt palms.

Wednesday of Holy Week was Spy Wednesday because on that day Judas made his deal with the enemies of Jesus to betray him for thirty pieces of silver. Hopefully, Holy Week was not too early or that spring had not come too late, because we had to eat dandelion greens these days of Holy Week so that the mosquitoes would not bite us during the coming summer. Just how this tradition got into our family I will never know. But follow it faithfully we did. Then we forgot all about it the following summer when we swapped at the zinging, biting mosquitoes while fishing at Brandon's Landing on Grand Lake.

Since our school followed the public school calendar, Holy Thursday was a school day. I do not remember that the early morning Mass for Holy Thursday was exceptional; certainly, there was no washing of feet in those days. But Good Friday was a Holy Day and a holiday, a day free from classes.

Good Friday meant the Black Fast. We could eat no meat or fish— I should say not!—nor eat anything that came from animals or fish. That meant no milk, no milk products, no eggs, nothing cooked or fried in lard.

So what was left? Coffee, teas, bread, bean soup (without pork condiments), natural fruits.AND STRAWBERRY JAM. Can you imagine that? Strawberry jam! We loved Good Fridays!

In those days we still did not have our own strawberry patch. Around the end of May, as the school days were coming to a close, we trooped out across the countryside in search of wild strawberries. It was not a blind search, because we knew from last year where the patches were, alongside Ashman's creek, in Feltz's woods, in our own orchard.

We used tin gallon cans. Wild strawberries are quite small. It is not easy to fill a gallon can, especially as we walked in the hot sun, the berries shook down and squeezed together and melted into a red bleeding glob at the bottom of the bucket. There was even less content when the green stems were picked off. So a bright red jar of wild strawberry jam was quite a prize.

Mom protected the few jars of strawberry jam in the cellar with her life. Only for most special visitors for a Sunday evening supper would Mom send one of us kids down to the cellar to bring up a jar of strawberry jam. From our benches at table, we watched our visitors spread their bread with our precious jam. After prayers, as the old folks continued talking in the front room, we swooped down upon the leftover jam like buzzards.

Yet on Good Friday, strawberry jam and freshly baked homemade bread fulfilled all the conditions of the Black Fast. What a delight to follow strictly the letter of the law, to feel holy and still enjoy the good things of life.

Three Hours Devotions meant just that: THREE HOURS. From twelve noon until three in the afternoon. Not two hours, not two and a half hours. Three hours. The first hour was not so bad: a reading of the Passion narrative and the priest performing a rite called the Mass of the Pre-Sanctified. But that left two hours to go. The Way of the Cross.Some long preaching. Rosaries. Anything to fill up the time.

It was not that we were indifferent to the mysteries being celebrated. Indeed, we became quite closely identified with our suffering Lord. Nature often followed the moods of the liturgical week. Good Friday would be dark, rainy, gloomy. Saturday had a little sunshine. And Easter Sunday a spring day of pure joy.

The Three Hours were sacred. One year we came out of church and saw that some building material had arrived at the Adoph Tumbusch house under construction next to the ball diamond. Mom was sure the house would be cursed because no one should work during the Three Hours.

After church, at home, Dad heard a baseball game on the radio. That was also a no-no. So we quietly enjoyed our strawberry jam and bread.

In those days Holy Saturday service was a half-secret service that the priest, a few servers and Teacher Eifert performed early in the morning. The people came around 8 a.m. when the actual Mass took place and the first Alleluia would be sung.

When was the end of Lent? We had to know, because we were waiting to get at all that candy we had hoarded for forty days. The church formally declared that Lent ended at twelve o'clock noon on Holy Saturday.

Dad was an excellent liturgical theologian. His opinion was that Lent ended with the early morning service because then we had sung Alleluia. But we had to play it safe. We followed the public law of the church.

So we got out our caches of candies and waited. At the first stroke of the noon Angelus Church bell from Cassella we ate our first piece of candy. Alleluia! The Lord is risen!

It took me many years to come to a full realization of what the dust of Ash Wednesday was all about. Remember you are dust and into dust you shall return. The solemn reminder of our common mortality.

But let us all have the patience to wait it all out a little longer. We shall return to the resurrected dust of the Lord. This very dust will be eternally glorified. Let us think about that a little bit.

It makes this piece of candy taste very good indeed.

39.
Hedge Fences

In Heaven, when I meet my grandfather, Christoph Ranly, I will tell him: "Grandpa. You did wonderful things in your life. You left us a great patri-mony in the farm, the buildings, the land. But you made two wagers which were bummers. Catalpa trees and hedge fences."

Both were quite literally unique to the Ranly farm. We knew very few catalpa groves like ours. And no one had hedge fences like the Ranlys.

Grandpa Ranly planted three acres of catalpa trees behind the chicken house in coordinated rows, five feet apart, like we used to plant our corn fields, so that the rows could be cultivated horizontally or vertically. With rows so close together the trees grew as straight as telephone poles, with all the branches, leaves and flowers at the very top. That was the whole idea. The tall, thin, straight trunks were to be cut up into fence posts.

But the harvest never came. We ourselves used precious few of the catalpa trees for fence posts. They served well as posts, for they were literally as straight as fence posts and so lightweight one could nail staples into them very easily. Did I say STAPLES? No, I wrote STAPLES, but I meant to say STEEPLES, because in our language those U-shaped nails were called steeples.

No one ever cut catalpa trees to market them as fence posts. Even Dad came to prefer steel fence posts. So while the catalpa grove served as a wonderful windbreak against winter winds sweeping in from the west, the trees themselves began to age and fall, one by one, criss-crossed between the straight rows.

Those fallen trunks, cut into cordwood, made excellent firewood for the heatrola in the sitting room. They burned a slow, yellow flame, gave off a steady heat and burned themselves into pure fly ash. Catalpa firewood left very little ashes to dispose of.

The catalpa grove had one week of glory, around the first week of June, when as in dress rehearsal, all the trees burst out into bloom at once. The flowers appeared on a cone shaped stem, like a small Christmas tree, with some ten/twelve blossoms on each stem. Each flower was like a snapdragon. You squeezed it on the side and it opened up like a lion's mouth in a circus cage.

Best of all was the aroma. The whole grove became a walk-in greenhouse with the sweetness of honey. The trees were alive with countless honey bees, bumble bees, yellow jackets, all working over the blossoms in search of that sweet nectar.

Don't we know how sweet it was! We picked each blossom very carefully from its stem. Then we sucked the bottom end of the flower. With luck, our mouth glowed with a taste like that of cotton candy, a whisper of sweetness that left us breathless. It was more of a promise, an intimation, of what a simple sensation of pure sweetness could become.

By late August the flowers became long green pods, like footlong green beans. Why we called them "fiddles" I cannot say. We took one long bean and stroked a shorter bean across it, as if we were stroking a bow across a violin.

After a few hard frosts, the catalpa beans turned brown. Over the winter, they dropped their beans for seed and, sure enough, in the spring small seedlings would appear in the lawn alongside the hog lane where a few special catalpa trees formed a kind of promenade.

You know, Grandpa Ranly, as a working cash crop, your catalpa grove was a complete flop. But your catalpa trees added a very distinctive element to our home place. For that we are grateful.

But why the hedge fence? Did you get that idea from Germany? The idea that ossage orange could be planted so closely together that they would form a fence tight enough to hold in cattle and swine?

Like the catalpa, an ossage orange tree standing alone can develop into a circular shade tree, very attractive. Its fruit is called ossage orange and it is the size and shape of a large orange, but green, turning into yellow, with a surface like a miniature bee cone. The fruit is as hard as a softball and oozes a white, gooey, icky milk. We threw them at one another in war games under the pretense that they were hand grenade bombs. Certainly, they were heavy and dangerous as missiles.

Grandpa's idea of a fence was to plant ossage orange bushes eight to ten inches apart. Then as the plants grew to a height of five to six feet, they were to be carefully trimmed. And, voila! You have a perpetually green fence, a haven to countless birds, a refuge for rabbits and ground hogs.

The final selling point of this miracle bush was that it had thorns. Every branch and every twig had thorns: short, sharp penetrating. So, of course, a carefully trimmed hedgerow would hold off cattle and pigs because of the thorns. Finally, perhaps, the idea was protection against erosion.

The largest line of hedge fence stretched from the southwest edge of our land. It followed the contours of the creek across the bottom ends of two fields and then came all the way up the second field to the bridge in the lane. It did serve as a protection against high water. Then there were smaller hedge rows east of the orchard and, for some time, even east of the garden.

One problem was trimming. By the time I was a boy, the hedge fences were quite old and had a tremendous vitality. By early summer, they could be virtual trees. Cutting back the new growth was an endless and difficult task.

In the garage (or smokehouse) we always had several long handled clippers which were known as hedge fence clippers. At times, the men needed saws and axes. Trimming hedge fences was a task of early spring. Large piles of cut brush were burned. I used to imagine that these brightly burning brush fires helped warm up the earth to bring on spring.

But, Grandpa, you haven't heard the worst part about your damnable hedge fences. The thorns! What we called stickers. Hedge fence stickers were a permanent and ubiquitous curse, a constant plague, the snake in paradise. For, of course, since May 11 (Mom's birthday) we ran barefoot until the beginning of school.

How many stickers were pulled out of bleeding feet! Loretta (Sister Teresa Joseph) learned her nursing skills by tending to our feet battered by hedge fence stickers. There was something perverse, almost diabolical, how hedge fence stickers could appear in the most unlikely places, like land mines, and penetrate a big toe or stick to a tender heel.

But they also helped us to bring on one of the biggest braggadocios of our Ranly family lore. Who had the toughest feet by the end of summer? There were the "I dare you!" barefoot races over gravel. But the biggest brag was: "I can run barefoot over hedge fence stickers and they can't hurt me!"

Dear Grandpa Ranly. Your catalpa grove is old, battered, but it is still there. But the hedge fences have long disappeared, pulled up by their roots and burned, all of them once and forever in some spring brush fires. The whole concept of fences has changed in modern mechanized, specialized farming. When every farm had milk cows, draught animals and pigs, the land was divided into many smaller fields. Every field needed secure fencing to keep the animals enclosed.

As we have noted, Robert Frost said about stone fences in his native New England that "Good fences make good neighbors." Stray cows and breakaway pigs make mad neighbors. But nowadays, cattle feeding lots and massive hog stables never permit animals—nor chickens—to graze on God's green earth. Grain farming has eliminated all fences. So the popular song of our youth "Don't Fence Me In" is now a reality in our part of western Ohio.

But I don't know. Even at the risk of stepping on a hedge fence sticker I would like to see just one more time a well-trimmed hedge fence along that south creek bank.

Grandpa Ranly. you worked hard to plant the hedge fence and kept it well trimmed. Today, even as a memory, it is in danger of disappearing.

40.
Spring

To hear frogs croak on Saint Patrick's Day meant that spring had sprung and we are to have a good summer. Actually, what we heard in early spring are called pipers or peepers It was not the deep croak of the bull frog which later in the summer we heard while fishing at Brandon's Landing.

The first crocuses peeping through the snow can be false prophets of spring. Some years even the yellow daffodils were covered with snow. The one who announced seeing the first robin redbreast was looked on with envy. We could have frost until the first week of May, the feast of some northern European saints who are called the "Icemen"—EISENMÄNNER. But, as Rodgers and Hammerstein sang about June, there came that undeniable moment when spring was coming. "It is coming, by gum, you can feel it it in the breeze, you can see it in the trees, look around, look around, look around!"

Spring means gardening, the earlier the better. Our major vegetable garden ran from the house to the barn, on the east side of the sidewalk, when there were still a few catalpa trees there. The lawn south of the house sloped down to the garden in a rather steep grade. Cutting grass on that slope was quite a task with our iron push mower.

The garden was about five yards wide, with a dirt path on both sides and a number of transverse paths. The rest of the area was in early potatoes, with maybe a few rows of sweet corn.

The first little patch of gardening was always lettuce, then radishes. Then peas, green beans, red beets, tomatoes and so on. When company came they examined the garden like judges at the county fair. A good or bad garden could make or break a family's reputation. That's why Rita and the Flautes keep their garden in back of the house where company can hardly find it. Why must company comment that the garden needs weeding?

Spring meant kite flying. We made our own kites, always a four-sided oblong star shape. One large stick, say, about two feet long. Then the shorter cross stick, tied together in the middle with white cord sting. The sticks were notched at ends and a string tied taut circled the four ends of the sticks. Brown wrapping paper (say, from a Sears Roebuck package) was pasted over this frame. We made paste out of wheat flour and water. Then we hunted for twine strings in the straw stack to make the kite's tale some fifteen feet long, with old rags and stockings.

Paul converted an old mechanized butter churn into a contraption to hold kite string. We had hundreds of feet of string and would let it all out as the wind lofted the kite up and away. We could wind all the string back with ease and speed.

March comes in like a lion and leaves like a lamb. In between there was every conceivable type of weather, but always with wind. March is the season for flying kites. We waited for a clear day and a steady wind. Not that strong a wind that made the tin roof on the machine shed rumble like thunder. Not a day with uneven gusts of wind. A day with a good steady wind.

It's best to have two people to set a kite flying, one to hold the kite against the wind and the other to run with the string until the kite takes off, soaring into the blue like a rocket with a ragtag tail. The strings tied to the four corners of the kite must be set very carefully or else the kite will zoom to the right or skirt to the left or nosedive straight into the ground. We had open fields all around us and so avoided trees and electric and telephone lines. The first kite of spring was better than a robin to reassure us that spring had come to stay.

We took kite flying very seriously. Sometimes we would try to test how long a kite would fly on its own. We left it out overnight and found it still flying in the morning. Even during passing snow showers an intrepid kite would hover in the sky, its tale flapping in the wind.

Sometimes we made tin cutouts with the shape of a man and a hook at the end. We tied a red handkerchief to the top of the tin. Then we hooked the tin onto the string of the kite, let the handkerchief billow out in the wind and the whole piece would climb up the string into the air towards the kite. A few hard shakes on the string loosened the hook and the contraption would fall to the ground like a man falling with a parachute. Try it sometime. It's great fun.

Summer began for the Ranlys on Ascension Thursday which was a family fishing day. Spring ended on May 11, Mom's birthday, when we were allowed to go barefoot.

God's in Heaven. All's in order.

41.
Fishing

The Ranlys would rather fish than eat, Mom often said. Put that in context. We are on a family fishing day at Brandon's Landing. Mom has set out the picnic lunch. No one in his right mind will refuse chicken fried with natural grease in an iron skillet, even when slightly cold. Nevertheless, there are priorities.

"But, Mom, I got a bite on my catfish line!" Yellow-belly catfish bite slow during the heat of the noon sun. And they are elusive and tricky and deserve close attention. So the choice between watching a fish line with a catfish bite or eating potato salad with pre-fried chicken is a protracted agonized decision.

Mom seemed to say that our fishing genes came from the Ranly line. But her own family were also great fishers. And Mom had that one great story about when she and Dad were alone on a boat. She was catching crappies one after another. Dad none. They switched poles. Mom continued to catch crappies. They switched sides of the boat. Mom caught crappies. Fish stories.

Do they tell fish stories in Heaven? Or does Heaven allow only the bare facts and nothing but the facts? How dull that would be!

Fish worms made up the basic, normal bait. We had our selected spots for digging fish worms: north of the chicken house or below big rocks in the hog lane. But the most reliable spot was next to the slop barrel on the east side of the hog stable. There the ground was always damp and soft. Those long shoestring-like worms would wiggle and twist when we palmed them and tossed them into the tin can. The bottom half of the can would be a squirming mass of worms which was then covered over with soft, damp ground.

In its own way, seining for minnows and crawdads in the creek was more fun than fishing. We carried all our bait with us from home. To have to buy bait—say, minnows—seemed like an admission of incompetence.

Over time, new technology and modernization began to affect even our style of fishing. At some point in history, Art made his famous declaration that fishing worms had become obsolete.

Fishing is fun only when it is taken seriously. The excitement of tomorrow's early rising to go fishing would keep us awake at night. Sometimes in bed I still have hallucinations over fishing. I see vividly a fishing cork jumping, running, submerging. The corks I see are the very corks we actually used in those days.

Catfish. When heavy rains sent the water over the banks of the creek, we began to calculate our timing. We got to the White Bridge just as these high waters were passing into the reservoir, that is, Grand Lake. The fresh water brought the channel catfish up the channels to feed in the muddy fresh waters.

We needed extra-heavy sinkers, even iron nuts and bolts, to keep the fish lines deep in the moving waters. But, oh, how beautiful are those blue, silvery channel catfish, with their flat mouths, beady eyes and large whiskers. But take care! They have sharp teeth and dangerous horns.

Crappies spawn in the shallows during the second or third warm week in May. They are temperamental. Sometimes you find them cooperative, sometimes not. We have a short pole with a small active cork. The minnow bait is set only a foot or so below the water. Then we work the line in and out of flags, near brush, alongside trees lying in the water. When all conditions are correct, like the Apostles with the Lord, one can make some miraculous catches of crappies.

Carp have received a bad press. Taken from the fresh waters of early spring they are quite tasty. One soon discovers how those little y-bones lie across the meat above the backbone. The y-bones are picked out, one by one, and then the soft, flaky meat of the carp can be eaten with ease.

Carp spawn in shallow waters so that at times they follow overflow waters into nearby fields. Sometimes we went after them with pitchforks. The best weapon was a big tin tub without a bottom. We dropped the tub upon the carp, wiggling about in the shallow water. Then we caught the carp by hand and threw them into a gunny sack. These carp we fed to the hogs.

Catching carp makes good stories. We rolled up the whites of bread to make dough-ball bait. We usually had a few carp lines out to keep things interesting. Especially if nothing else was biting, we tried to see how many and how large carp we could catch.

One time we were fishing in two boats in the high green rushes called flags. Although we were quite close, the flags were so thick we could not see the people in the other boat. So we began lofting carp up and over the high flags from one boat into the other boat. Catching more carp became a big order for self-defense and retaliation in the on-going war.

Some of the best fish stories are not about the ones who got away, but what we did when the fish were not biting.

A good technique on a quiet day was to lift anchor out over the lake and drift with the wind, with fish lines out. If a few fish were caught in quick succession, the anchor was dropped with the expectation that we had come upon a school of feeding fish. Then we fished that spot for a longer period of time, testing out our luck.

On a particular day since early morning, fishing was very slow. Disgusted and impatient, Art said: "School of fish! These dumb fish don't go to school! The next fish we catch, we smell its breath. If it has liquor on his breath, we throw in the anchor, because we know we have come upon a tavern. That's where the fish are: drinking at a bar, not going to school."

On another slow day we were fishing from the banks of a channel. To our great annoyance, we were catching little red-bellied turtles, called stinkpots. Such turtles are classified as pests. Each turtle lost its head to a sharp knife.

Don fell asleep, slumped up against a willow tree. We lifted his pole out of the water and set the fish hook into the bloody neck of a headless turtle. We then put the line back into the water, shouting: "Don! You got a bite!"

Startled, Don pulled in his line. "Another damn turtle. But wait! It's a headless turtle! How did a headless turtle bite on my line?"

Paul for all his life, and now in retirement, has remained the most dedicated fisher of the family. Now that most of the family are retired, there are well-organized week-long fishing trips to Rice Lake, Ontario. We do only pan fishing.

I say Paul takes his fishing seriously. Among other things, he brings along a pair of binoculars. He studies other fishers in other boats to see what they are catching, what bait they use, how big are the fish.

We are taking a long noonday rest at the cabin. But not Paul. He is on the dock with his binoculars, looking out over the lake. Ralph calls over to Paul's wife, resting in the shade of the cabin porch. "Marie. Watch that man of yours. He's looking at some bare-breasted girls down there on the beach."

"Not to worry. If they are not catching fish, Paul won't bother."

42.
Mom

Sophia Speck married Peter Ranly on May 1, 1912, when the bride was eighteen years old. All her life, Mom talked against a teen-age marriage to all her daughters. She had nothing against the many of us who filled up her life. But I think she felt she lost a part of her youth and was plunged into the daily responsibilities of marriage and motherhood too early.

Mom's family name SPECK in German means BACON. During her wedding (I was told) there were any number of jokes about Pete Ranly getting himself a piece of bacon. Or, as we would say today, Dad was bringing home the bacon.

We were a Catholic family in a thoroughly Catholic setting. There are books and stories and movies and TV serials about any number of national groups and religions in the American experience. Largely because of two World Wars there is precious little in the broad American culture about a very significant group throughout the United States: the German Catholic community.

We were a Catholic family. At one time we sported three Priests and one Sister. Yet none of us ever studied in a Catholic school—strictly speaking. We did not know Catholic Sisters. Mom was far ahead of us. Her teachers for the first years of primary school were Sisters of the Precious Blood.

West central Ohio remains predominantly Catholic because of the permanent presence since 1844 of the missionary Congregation of the Precious Blood. Father Francis de Sales Brunner founded some eight convents/mission houses on the Indiana/Ohio boarder to minister to the Catholic immigrant families.

One of these convents—Himmelgarten ("Garden of Heaven")—was less than a mile from where Mom was born. The Precious Blood Sisters taught in the one-room public school down the road. I think Mom was infected with a religious vocation by these Sisters. All of us received the Faith from her in our very genes.

The convent closed and the Sisters moved on, but Mom stayed on to complete all eight grades in what was called Home School. She always told us that she played with her class in a championship softball game on the last day of school.

While Dad had administrative and secretarial skills, Mom's forte was a dogged practicality. She could prepare daily meals for a dozen or more hungry mouths, supervise the weekly laundry, darn socks, mend clothes. She was a better than average seamstress, especially in sewing girls' dresses, jumpers and blouses.

When Mom sat down to write, she worked laboriously with her large left arm, spelling words more by sound than by the dictionary. (She always wrote KNOW for NO.) But her short letters were rich with wisdom, wry comments and solid advice. My brothers in the service and those of us in Religious life cherished every one of Mom's letters as a precious personal gift. I feel sorry for those around home who never received a written letter from Mom. For all her limitations in writing skills, I think she expressed herself better in writing than in speaking.

Mom never lost interest in life and all its aspects. Hers was a deeply personal interest and not only a passing curiosity.

For several summers she accompanied me as my "priest's cook" as I substituted for vacationing priests in rural parishes of the Midwest. After the Sunday service, for the rest of the six days of the week, there was little to do. I brought along books to continue my studies and writing.

At Sanford, Wisconsin, I told Mom I was going to the library, that there was nothing for her to do, that I would be back for lunch. She insisted on coming along. So I directed her to the reading room. She found the periodical rack and a few hours later I had to drag her away from her new-found reading material.

Another time in a Wisconsin town, I left her in the parked car. When I returned she was in a serious conversation with a Native American in feather headdress. This was more than a tourist asking someone to pose for a picture. Mom and the stranger were talking like long lost relatives.

A priest friend of mine always told me that Mom saved his mother's life. The two women met at Saint Charles Seminary on Visiting Sunday. Within minutes Mom had the lady analyzed and convincingly counseled her towards retaking calm responsibility over her life.

Mom was like that. Not bullying, not imperious, but straightforward and always right. That is why neighbor ladies and members of sewing circles and prayer groups so cherished Mom's presence and advice.

Mom enjoyed a good joke as well as anyone, be it a practical joke played against one of us or simply a good tale. When we were planning to put in an indoor bathroom in our log house—what is this modern world coming to!—it was explained that there must be a pipe from the toilet bowl through the roof as a kind of escape valve for moisture and unwanted smells. Mom wondered out loud if there would be a whistle on the top of the pipe so that every time one would let a really loud one go, the pipe whistle would blow. Hearing this from Mom we thought was quite risqué, but she thoroughly enjoyed the silly cleverness of her own thought. Secretly, we thought the idea was very funny indeed.

I was doing monthly parish accounts the first summer that Mom was with me as "priest's cook." So I gave her forty-five dollars in payment for her services. She was embarrassed and adamant in refusing the money. "Ach! What is this? I am here. I have a bed. We eat. What else is there?"

I explained to her that I must leave financial accounts for the returning pastor and his parish council and that, of course, the pastor paid this monthly salary to his housekeeper. The books must show the same movement of money.

Slowly her reluctance melted into a personal, pleasurable pride. Later, she triumphantly explained to family and friends. "For the first time in my life I worked!"

Indeed! When a culture values only the paycheck, Mom who never was paid with money in her life, could feel that she never worked.

She gave birth to sixteen living children, reared thirteen of us, managed a farming family for almost fifty years, but only with forty-five dollar wages in her hand could she declare: "This is the first time in my life I worked!"